GARDENERS' WORLD

PLANTS FOR SMALL GARDENS

GARDENERS' WORLD

PLANTS FOR SMALL GARDENS

SUE FISHER

BBC BOOKS

PICTURE CREDITS

GARDEN PICTURE LIBRARY pages 9 (John Glover), 19 (Brigitte Thomas), 33 (John Miller), 52–3 (Brigitte Thomas), 97 (Clive Nichols) and 115 (John Glover); PHOTOS HORTICULTURAL pages 7, 21, 25, 27, 28, 40, 44, 57, 59, 69, 70, 76 (left), 89, 99, 107, 110 and 117. The remaining photographs were taken for the BBC by JOHN JEFFORD and details of the gardens shown are as follows: Capel Manor Horticultural Centre, Enfield, Middlesex pages 38, 54, 76 (right) and 105; Mr & Mrs Davis, Capricorner, Quainton, Bucks page 94; Anne Dexter, 23 Beechcroft Road, Oxford pages 48, 72, 79 and 101; Mr & Mrs Elliot, 56 Windmill St, Brill, Bucks pages 10–11, 61 and 82; Lucy Gent, 24 Grove Terrace, Kentish Town, London NW5 page 86; Mr & Mrs Hulton, 70 Gloucester Crescent, Camden Town, London NW1 pages 47 and 85; Sheila Jackson, Flat 1, 1F Oval Road, Camden Town, London NW1 pages 98 and 103; Lady Jocelyn, 54 Burnfoot Avenue, London SW6 pages 42, 93 and 96; Anthony Noel, 17 Fulham Park Gardens, London SW6 pages 15, 37, 65 and 67; Waterers Landscapes, London Road, Windlesham, Surrey pages 22, 121 and 124

All the gardens, with the exception of Capel Manor Horticultural Centre and Waterers Landscapes, are open to the public under the National Gardens Scheme.

Published by BBC Books,
a division of BBC Enterprises Limited,
Woodlands, 80 Wood Lane, London W12 0TT

First published 1993

ISBN 0 563 36301 0

Set in 10/13pt Kennerley by Ace Filmsetting Ltd, Frome
Printed and bound in Great Britain by Clays Ltd, St Ives Plc
Colour separations by Dot Gradations Ltd, Berkhamsted
Cover Printed by Clays Ltd, St Ives Plc

CONTENTS

INTRODUCTION

Gardening in a limited space – be it a modern, small garden, courtyard, patio area or tiny, front garden – is no bar to having a wealth of colourful and attractive plants, but it is necessary to be selective about which ones to have. At no time in the past has there been such an enormous variety of plants readily available through garden centres and other sources, but such unlimited choice can sometimes be a mixed blessing when space is at a premium.

My choice of plants for a small space is most influenced by two factors. The first is eventual size; few things are more heart-breaking than doing constant battle with any plant intent on garden domination, so anything that grows too large hasn't been included here. Plant vigour has to be taken into account too; invasive varieties have been excluded or warned against, as something that grows exuberantly in a large garden can become a downright pest when it has to be restricted. The second factor is whether the plant will 'earn its keep' in ornamental terms and look good for as long as possible relating to the amount of space it occupies. Because a tree, for example, is a major feature, it's of little value in the small garden if it produces a spectacular burst of flowers for only a couple of weeks and is horridly dull for the rest of the year. Other attributes such as fruit or attractive foliage are needed to extend the period of interest. This factor is most important for the large plants that usually form the backbone of a garden – typically trees and shrubs.

Above all this book is a personal choice of plants that I consider are amongst the best performers for a small garden. There's something here to satisfy all levels of interest and experience – easy to grow and less usual varieties as well as a number of the newest introductions. Where relevant, the largest groups of plants have been separated according to the factors foremost in importance to their selection: with climbers, for example, the amount of sun or shade that a wall or fence receives is the crucial factor influencing which plant can be grown on a given site. They are therefore grouped

A mixed group of a dozen different plants in a small space provides enormous interest; early summer colour comes from the bold lime-green flowers of *Euphorbia wulfenii*, small clumps of pink, red and white helianthemums, and a stunning blue *Ceanothus* on the wall.

according to their preferences for shady, sunny, or very sunny, sheltered sites. Similarly, conifers are grouped according to habit and size; alpines according to where they should be planted.

Each individual description is accompanied by details on any cultural likes or dislikes, though unless stated otherwise the plants selected here are easy to grow. There are also many useful planting suggestions, such as how to create attractive associations with other plants, plus there are short features throughout the book highlighting plants for particular uses such as attracting wildlife. The plants are listed botanical name first, under which they will be listed in catalogues and garden centres when you come to purchase. This is followed by their common name.

Creating a beautiful environment, however tiny, can be enormously satisfying and relaxing – and especially therapeutic in today's fast-paced world. If you have a new plot, don't be put off by the mystique that sometimes appears to surround gardening. Choosing the right plant for the right place, along with a little basic preparation and care, is all it takes to have a flourishing garden and a rewarding interest that can last a lifetime. If you're already a gardener, I hope this book helps you discover even more wonderful plants to enrich your garden.

1

PLANNING FOR PLANTS

One of the most important steps in designing a garden is selecting plants that like the conditions your garden can offer. Opinions may be divided over whether plants can communicate or not, but they certainly have their likes and dislikes; if you put them somewhere unsuitable, they'll let you know by sulking or dying! Before you even start thinking what to buy, a little time spent on site and soil analysis can save you disappointment, money, and will result in a much more flourishing and labour-saving garden.

SOIL pH

It is vital to know whether your soil is acid or alkaline, as this can affect the health of certain plants such as rhododendrons, which are acid-lovers that sicken and die on alkaline soil. Soil pH is measured on a scale from 1 (acid) to 14 (alkaline or limy); most soils are between 4 and 8, and the ideal level for most plants is 6.5 (slightly acid). You can check your soil pH using a cheap and simple soil testing kit.

Although you can make acid soil more alkaline by adding lime, it's a waste of time and money trying to do the reverse. In a garden with alkaline soil, it is therefore best to grow acid-loving plants in tubs or raised beds in suitably acid topsoil or compost.

SOIL TYPE

It is also necessary to identify your soil type – whether it's sandy, chalky, clay or loam – as this influences plant growth too. Sandy soil, for example, is light and free-draining, ideal for plants that like drier conditions, whereas moisture-loving plants would suffer badly from lack of water. (Details on improving soil appear on page 14.)

ASPECT

The aspect, or direction, that a site faces affects how much sun or shade the site receives. South- and, to a lesser extent,

Where space is limited, it's important to place bright colours, such as these red and pink astilbes, in the foreground – bright colours at the end of the garden would immediately catch the eye and so make it appear shorter.

west-facing borders are sunny and warm, whereas north- and east-facing sites are shady and cooler. Other factors such as overhanging trees and nearby buildings also affect the sunniness of a site.

Choosing suitable plants for the aspect of a site also increases the likelihood of securing the best plant combinations and overall appearance for your borders. Plants that like the same conditions tend to look good together: sun-loving plants such as lavender, rosemary and cistus make a harmonious combination with grey-leaved plants, for example.

PLANT HARDINESS

A great many of the plants that we can buy today have originated from countries with widely differing climates. Those from much warmer countries often will not tolerate frost; thus a plant's hardiness must be considered when deciding whether – and where – to plant it. The amount of exposure also needs to be assessed – tough, hardy plants are needed on exposed, windy sites. At the other extreme, gardens in cities are very sheltered and therefore particularly suitable for less hardy plants. The best way to get a feel for what grows well in your area is to look at plants in nearby gardens and talk to the staff at your local garden centre.

Plants with colourful foliage have long-lasting appeal; golden plants give this border a real lift, and include golden marjoram, *Spiraea* 'Goldflame', *Euonymus* 'Emerald 'n' Gold' and *Lonicera* 'Baggesen's Gold'.

The relative hardiness of a plant has been indicated where appropriate, though unless you want a totally trouble-free garden it's often worth living slightly dangerously by growing plants that may only just be able to tolerate the cold in your area, for the extra beauty and slightly exotic flavour they add to the garden – it's the luck of the draw whether a severe winter will arrive to decimate your plants or not. There are always safeguards: cuttings taken the previous summer can be overwintered indoors, or for total security plants can be grown in pots and overwintered in a greenhouse or conservatory.

COLOUR AND INTEREST ALL YEAR ROUND

Many small gardens are on view from indoors all year and are almost part of the house, so having something looking good right through the year is of paramount importance. The best way to create an all-year garden is to combine different types of plants – shrubs, roses, perennials, conifers, and so on – to make a mixed border that looks colourful and interesting all year. Even fruit and vegetables can be incorporated: *The Ornamental Kitchen Garden* by Geoff Hamilton (BBC Books, 1990) shows how to grow fruit and vegetables together with ornamental plants in your garden.

The key to having mixed borders looking good all year is careful selection of plants to give a succession of colour and interest. Whatever the time of year you can find some plant in flower, and there are other ways of obtaining attractive and long-lasting colour – using foliage for example. Foliage is a major asset that is often overlooked but is immensely important; after all, it's there for at least half the year, far longer than the most persistent flowers. Many plants possess coloured, variegated or attractively shaped leaves, and even the less flamboyant leaves still have different textures and subtle shades of green – the most dominant yet restful of nature's colours, which shouldn't be forgotten when building up the overall picture. There are also fruit- and berry-bearing plants to make a lovely autumn and winter display. Other plants have leaves that develop gorgeous autumn tints, and a few bear colourful stems or attractive bark for winter interest.

When deciding which plants to choose, don't just go along to the garden centre unprepared – all those tempting displays can seduce even the most hardened gardener. It's best to plan in advance, making a separate list for each season or each month to ensure that you have a succession of colour. Start by listing suitable plants looking good in winter, the least colourful time of year, and work backwards, rather than starting in spring when there are stacks of tempting plants. First priority should be large permanent plants that form the 'skeleton' of the garden, such as trees and shrubs, then you can infill with smaller plants such as perennials, grasses and small shrubs. The large plants will need to be sufficiently well spaced to allow for future growth, so a newly planted garden can look quite gappy. Fill these gaps with short-lived plants such as drifts of cheap and easily grown annuals, or perennials that will transplant happily when necessary.

THE ART OF PLANTING

An old gardener once told me there are no clashes in nature. Perhaps she was thinking of wild flowers, because with garden plants there's potential for some hideous combinations! Colour is a very personal matter – some people like softer shades, others prefer bright, bold colours. Whatever your preferences, it's worth planning a rough colour scheme for your borders. When in doubt, aim for simplicity and restrict the number of colours in a border, rather than having too many and ending up with a 'liquorice allsorts' effect. One important point to remember is that bright colours 'advance' whereas paler colours 'recede', so don't place brightly coloured plants at the far end of the garden or border, or they'll immediately catch the eye and make the distance appear shorter.

Colour is only one part of the equation when planting; shape, form and texture affect the appearance of a border all year. The most common mistake is to put plants of a similar shape together, which tends to give a uniformly dull appearance with no contrast. However, several rounded plants broken up by a clump of bold, spiky foliage and fronted with a carpet of prostrate plants, for example, looks far more interesting. The same principles can be used to perk up an existing border – just replacing a few plants with others of contrasting shape can effect an amazing transformation.

BUYING YOUR PLANTS

Most plants are sold in containers by nurseries and garden centres. Standards can vary enormously, so it's worth bearing a few points in mind when buying. Plants should look healthy: avoid any that are very dry, have lots of dead or discoloured foliage, any sign of pests or disease, or are surrounded by weeds. Watch out for 'potbound' plants that have been there too long and have packed their pots with roots. This severely checks their growth and, apart from perennials, they'll never really recover. Perennials may be rejuvenated by dividing their rootstock in autumn or early spring.

All plants should be clearly labelled with their full botanical name. Avoid those with just a generic name – 'aster', for example – as their quality could be variable. Beware newspaper adverts offering miraculous plants identified by only a common name and which rarely live up to their sales pitch.

Most plants in this book should be available from good nurseries and garden centres. However, less usual plants may have to be obtained from specialist nurseries, many of which offer a mail order service (see page 126).

2

PLANTING AND AFTERCARE

No matter how good your plants are, the amount of attention paid to soil preparation, planting and aftercare has the greatest influence on their eventual success.

SOIL PREPARATION

All soils benefit from some preparation before planting, particularly if you have a newly built house or immature garden. Light, free-draining soils such as sand and chalk need plenty of organic matter to improve their water and nutrient-holding capacity. Heavy clay soils should be broken up and made more free-draining; it's best to dig the ground to two spades' depth in autumn and leave the soil in large lumps over winter for the frost to break down, then in spring work in coarse grit and organic matter.

'Organic matter' may be one of several materials. Manure is ideal and contains some nutrients, but must be well rotted – preferably at least a year old. Mushroom compost is a good soil conditioner contain-ing a few nutrients; however, it contains some lime so isn't suitable for acid-loving plants. Garden compost is ideal. If you haven't got a compost heap I recommend starting one immediately, as all garden and kitchen waste is a valuable potential source of plant food. A variety of composts can be purchased ready packaged. I avoid using peat on environmental grounds, so I choose an alternative such as those based on coco-nut fibre or other recycled materials.

PLANTING

Although container-grown plants may be planted at any time of the year, certain times are more beneficial than others. Never plant when the ground is frozen or waterlogged – you won't be doing your soil or your plants any favours. Deciduous plants such as trees,

Good soil preparation is particularly important where plants will be densely packed. This town garden is crammed with foliage plants, including hostas peeping over a box hedge. Lilies in pots add a splash of delicate colour.

shrubs and roses are best planted in autumn when the soil is warm and moist; they'll start making root growth immediately and continue to establish in mild periods through the winter, ready for an explosion of growth in the spring. Because evergreens keep their leaves all year, they're more susceptible to cold, drying winter winds and frosts. Therefore the safest time to plant these is spring as the weather is warming up, so they have plenty of time to establish before winter; alternatively plant them in early autumn, provided the weather isn't hot and dry. In exposed sites newly planted evergreens benefit from a temporary windbreak of polythene or fine netting for the first year.

PLANTING TECHNIQUES

Several golden rules apply for all plants. Always give them a good watering several hours before planting; this is particularly important in spring and summer. Dig a hole larger than the plant's rootball and mix some compost, enriched with a handful of slow-release fertilizer such as bonemeal, into the hole and with the soil for backfilling. Garden compost is ideal, or use one of the many different, ready-packaged, planting composts, some of which already contain fertilizer so extra bonemeal will not be needed.

Remove the pot carefully from container-grown plants, disturbing the roots as little as possible; to minimize disruption, very large plants are best placed in the hole first and the pot is then cut off. If the roots have wound around inside the pot, spread them out in the planting hole – don't try and squeeze them into it or they'll become deformed, so the plant will never grow properly and may become unsteady. Make sure the top of the rootball is at ground level, then backfill with the prepared soil, keeping the plant upright and firming the soil as you go. Finally tread firmly all around the plant, leaving a shallow depression around the base to gather the maximum amount of rainwater; then give the plant a good watering immediately.

To plant trees and shrubs that may have been purchased rootballed, with their roots wrapped in sacking, place the rootball in the hole and just cut away the top and sides of the sacking, leaving it in the hole to rot down. Some plants purchased by mail order may be bare rooted – keep these moist until conditions are right to plant, and soak them for 2 hours before planting. Rootballed and bare rooted plants are only sold during winter.

Trees need staking for several years after planting until they've put down a good network of roots. A short, stout stake protruding 0.6–1 m (2–3 foot) above the ground is best for a tree 1.8–2.4 m (6–8 foot) high, holding it secure but still encouraging it to make good root development. Knock the stake in after the planting hole has been dug, then plant the tree and secure it using a wide, plastic tree tie.

AFTERCARE

Lack of water in the first year is the most common reason for losing new plants, especially those planted in spring and summer. In dry weather new plants need regular soakings to keep them in good health, so if you're away on holiday make sure someone can do watering duty. Inspect plants at regular intervals, as wind and frost may loosen the soil around the roots so plants may need periodic firming. Check all ties are secure yet not too tight, especially on trees where ill-fitting ties can rub into the trunk. The soil around all plants should be kept clear of grass and weeds, which compete for valuable water and nutrients. All plants benefit from an annual feed of slow-release fertilizer in late winter or early spring. Annual mulching with garden compost or well-rotted manure also keeps the soil in good condition.

MULCHING

A mulch is a protective layer on top of the soil. It is one of the most effective aids to successful plant establishment as it conserves soil moisture and suppresses weed growth.

Various materials can be used as a mulch. Gravel looks attractive, particularly for dry, sunny sites where it makes a superb setting for sun-loving plants with bold foliage such as yuccas, and should be laid at least 5 cm (2 inches) thick. A single layer of black polythene or woven polypropylene is effective but unsightly, and needs to be disguised with soil or gravel. Mushroom compost is good and relatively cheap, and bark chippings are dearer and more ornamental. Mulches should always be laid on moist, weed-free soil; compost or bark mulches should be applied in a layer 5 cm (2 inches) thick.

3

TREES

Trees play a starring role in any garden. They help give it style and structure, soften the hard lines of buildings and walls, filter out noise and pollution, and with their grace and beauty help transform the smallest of gardens into a lush oasis sheltered from the outside world. Small gardens need trees to match, and, as even the smallest tree will eventually grow to become a major feature, it makes sense for trees to be the starting point when designing your planting.

Ultimate size has to be the overriding factor when choosing trees, as many are large varieties, which would rapidly take over a small plot. There are, however, numerous well-behaved trees which are suitable for the small garden, and eliminating large trees rigorously will reduce the list of possible varieties at once; out go most of the birch and beech family, poplars and many maples, along with a host of less common trees such as *Liriodendron* (tulip tree). As well as size, shape needs to be considered in relation to the space available. Although many trees form a typical round-headed shape, there are others that are narrow and columnar, wide-spreading, or have a head of branches weeping down to the ground.

Because trees will be the largest living elements in your garden, it's well worth remembering that, in ornamental terms, they have to 'earn their keep' more than most other plants. Trees can provide visual interest in many ways: flowers; attractively shaped or coloured foliage, fruit or berries; a burst of autumn leaf colour; or attractive bark for winter interest. If you've got room for several trees it's more beneficial to choose varieties that look good at different times of the year, rather than having one big, short burst of colour. Another way of adding interest to a tree is by training one of the less vigorous climbing plants, such as a clematis, up into the branches.

To gain full benefit from a tree it's neces-

Trees make outstanding features for any garden. In contrast to the many spring-flowering trees, *Prunus subhirtella* 'Autumnalis Rosea' (autumn cherry) flowers from late autumn through winter, and brightens the dullest of winter days.

sary to think carefully about its attributes in relation to its position in the garden. On a purely ornamental level a tree can be used as a focal point to catch the eye or just to give height and substance to a border along with other plants. Trees can serve a variety of practical uses too, giving privacy from over-looking windows or blocking out a blot on the landscape. But beware of falling into the trap of planting bigger and faster-growing trees for rapid screening – they won't obe-diently stop at the desired height but keep on growing, dominating your own and neighbouring gardens and often interfering with drains and foundations. Far better to be patient for a couple of years and have a tree in keeping with the rest of your garden.

When choosing a tree, the garden's soil and aspect should be taken into account. Most trees grow well in a wide range of soils but some do have particular likes or dislikes; unless otherwise stated, all the trees described here will grow in a whole variety of soils, preferably enriched with plenty of organic matter before planting. Compared with other garden plants, aspect isn't so important for a tree unless the site is unduly shady or sunny. As a general rule, however, trees grown primarily for flower do best in a reasonable amount of sun, whilst foliage trees tolerate a shadier site.

To help make your selection easier, trees are described in five sections: foliage; flow-ers; ornamental fruits or berries; weeping trees; and fruit trees. As many trees here

have more than one season of interest, they appear in the section relevant to their most ornamental feature. All the varieties described here should be obtainable as young, container-grown trees around 1.8–2.4 m (6–8 ft) high which are usually 2–3 years old. If you want to save a couple of years of growing time, it's possible to obtain some varieties during winter as larger 'bare-rooted' trees (lifted straight from their nursery field). These are aged from 3 years upwards, and therefore come in a range of sizes.

All sizes given below are those reached in approximately 10 years. Soil and aspect will affect the rate of growth, as will the amount of initial soil preparation, annual feeding and maintenance.

TREES FOR FOLIAGE

Foliage trees lack the flamboyant bursts of colour given by flowering trees, but they work their way to the gardener's heart by a more roundabout route. They look superb clothed in their draperies of fresh, spring leaves, provide a backcloth to the garden's burst of summer flowers, and finally take centre stage again in the less floriferous months of late summer and autumn; a few even provide winter colour. None of the trees described here are evergreen, but from spring to autumn their foliage makes a con-stant and untiring contribution to the overall picture of the garden.

My first choice of foliage tree for the small

garden has to be *Acer negundo* 'Flamingo'. Its delicate foliage makes a stunning display, conspicuously variegated pink, cream and pale green when young, the pink gradually fading through the summer. It forms an irregularly-shaped dome but can be kept more compact if pruned in summer; this also encourages more of the pink, young growths. Plant this excellent tree as a focal point especially if seen against the background of a dark hedge or fence; it is also superb grown with purple-leaved shrubs. Height 4.5 m (15 feet). *A.n.* 'Flamingo' is also sold in bush form, which looks wonderful underplanted with a carpet of dark-foliaged, winter-flowering heathers. It is best pruned in summer to maintain a bushy shape around 1.5 m (5 feet) high with a spread of 1.2 m (4 feet). Similar but not quite as spectacular are *A.n.* 'Elegans', with leaves margined bright yellow, and *A.n.* 'Variegatum', which has leaves edged with white. If any of these varieties produce shoots with plain green leaves, cut these out immediately. Height 4.5 m (15 feet).

The 'snakebark' maples are so-called because of their marbled and striated bark, which is shown off to its best against a dark background. They also possess attractive, large, lobed leaves. One of the loveliest is *A. grosseri* var. *hersii*, with olive-green leaves contrasting beautifully with the red leaf stalks and young stems; the leaves colour magnificently in shades of red and orange in autumn. The leaves of *A. pensylvanicum*

(moosewood) are pink on opening, then changing to fresh green, and finally turning bright butter-yellow in autumn. In winter the green-and-white, patterned bark of both varieties is revealed in its full glory. Both snakebarks form a fairly upright head of branches and dislike chalky soils and exposed sites. Height 3.6 m (12 feet).

Golden foliage brightens the dullest of days and provides a marvellous backdrop for a wide range of shrubs. *Robinia pseudoacacia* 'Frisia' (golden false acacia) makes an outstanding splash of colour with its feathery, bright yellow leaves in spring and summer, turning to rich old gold in autumn. Its

Acer pensylvanicum has unusual coloured bark which looks especially ornamental in winter.

rounded, fairly open head of branches tend to be brittle, however, so making it unsuitable for exposed, windy positions.

Purple makes a very striking contrast to gold but such dark-coloured trees can sometimes be a little overwhelming, so careful planning of the surrounding planting is needed to avoid any colour clashes. *Malus* 'Royalty' (purple crab apple) has glossy, deep purple leaves through spring and summer, which turn deep wine-red in autumn; crimson flowers in spring and dark red fruits in autumn are excellent bonuses. Height 4.5 m (15 feet).

A purple-leaved tree makes an attractive focal point. To its left the variegated leaves of *Cornus alba* 'Elegantissima' make a good contrast. On the right of the pond the attractive divided leaves of a Japanese maple associate especially well with the water.

FLOWERING TREES

Few sights are more breathtaking than trees covered with a glorious mass of flower. The problem with flowering trees, especially in spring, is that they can be a 2-week wonder if their flowers get whisked away by a strong wind. So for a small garden a flowering tree really needs other qualities for extra interest: attractive foliage, an interesting shape, ornamental fruits or autumn leaf colour – any of which will ensure your tree will look attractive for a good part of the year and really give you value for money.

One of the best all-rounders is *Amelanchier lamarckii* (snowy mespilus), a magnificent sight in spring covered with masses of white flowers mixed with the silky, young, coppery-red leaves, which colour to rich shades of red and orange in autumn. *A.* 'Ballerina' bears profuse quantities of larger white flowers. Amelanchiers can be grown easily in many situations from sandy to boggy soil, but give the best autumn colour on lime-free soils. Height 4.5 m (15 feet).

Crab apples are first-rate trees for the small garden, bearing masses of blossom in mid- to late spring followed by edible fruits in autumn. The small-garden varieties here have been chosen for their flowering qualities, but there are more crab apples in the sections on fruiting and weeping trees. *Malus* 'Evereste' has a neat, conical shape and bears masses of flowers, up to 5 cm (2 inches) across, red in bud opening to white and followed by orange-yellow fruits in autumn. *M.* 'Snowcloud' really lives up to its name when covered with large white flowers, which are semi-double to double, followed by light crops of yellow fruits. It has an upright habit. *M.* 'Van Eseltine' has an erect, almost columnar shape and is particularly good for planting in a border, where it makes a distinctive companion for a group of shrubs. Its large, semi-double flowers create a superb display, red in bud opening to shell-pink flushed with white, and are followed by yellow fruits in autumn. Height 4.5 m (15 feet).

M. floribunda (Japanese crab) is an exceptionally pretty tree and a fabulous sight in mid-spring, when the long, arching branches are smothered in flowers, dark red in bud opening to white flushed with pale pink. Small, red-and-yellow fruits follow in autumn. Its shape, however, is somewhat untidy and not particularly attractive in winter, so rather than planting it as a solitary specimen it's best in a border with other plants that provide interest at other times of the year. A lovely and less common variety is *M. coronaria* 'Charlottae', which flowers in late spring, slightly later than most crab apples. Its masses of large, shell-pink flowers smell deliciously of violets. Green fruits are borne in autumn, and as an extra bonus the large, lobed leaves colour richly in autumn too. Height 4.5 m (15 feet).

Spring-flowering cherries are a magnifi-

PLANTS TO ATTRACT WILDLIFE

Wild creatures such as birds, bees and butterflies add a whole new dimension to gardening with their beauty and interest. To create a user-friendly environment for wildlife, and so help redress the balance of their destroyed habitats in the wild, include a good proportion of beneficial plants – and water – in your garden. Even the tiniest garden can be transformed into a real wildlife haven. Incidentally birds virtually always prefer red and orange berries to other colours.

FRUIT/BERRY-BEARING PLANTS TO FEED BIRDS

Berberis (see page 49)

Cotoneaster (both trees and shrubs) (see pages 27 and 50)

Iris foetidissima (Gladwin iris) (see page 98)

Malus (crab apple) (see pages 27–8)

Pyracantha (firethorn) (see page 70)

Sorbus (see page 29)

FLOWERS TO ATTRACT BEES

Caltha palustris (kingcup or marsh marigold) (see page 123)

Caryopteris (see page 34)

Ceratostigma (see page 34)

Cotoneaster (see pages 27, 50, 68)

Daphne (see pages 43–4)

Echinops (globe thistle) (see page 86)

Foeniculum vulgare var. *purpureum* (bronze fennel) (see page 87)

Hebe (see page 36)

Hellebore (see page 97)

Lavandula (see page 36)

Limnanthes douglasii (poached-egg flower) (see page 114)

Malus (crab apple) (see pages 23, 27–8)

Nepeta (catmint) (see page 90)

Perovskia (Russian sage) (see page 38)

Pieris (see page 56)

Pyracantha (firethorn) (see page 70)

Rosmarinus (see page 38)

Salix (willow) (see pages 30 and 49)

Sarcococca (Christmas box) (see page 50)

Skimmia (see page 51)

Sorbus (see page 29)

Viburnum tinus and *V. opulus* 'Compactum' (see page 46)

FLOWERS TO ATTRACT BUTTERFLIES

Achillea (see page 87)

Aster (Michaelmas daisy) (see pages 92 and 94)

Clematis heracleifolia (see page 86)

Hesperis matronalis (dame's violet or sweet rocket) (see page 118)

Lavandula (see page 36)

Nepeta (catmint) (see page 90)

Scabious (see page 91)

Sedum spectabile (see page 90)

The flat heads of *Sedum spectabile*, a late summer-flowering perennial, are popular with butterflies. Three types of butterfly can be seen here – tortoiseshells, a peacock, and a red admiral in the background.

cent sight in full flower, but the majority don't really have a long enough period of interest for the small garden. Although many cherries, especially Japanese varieties, can be seen almost groaning under the weight of their spring blossoms, a good shower of rain and a strong wind tends to reduce their glory to something suspiciously resembling wet toilet paper. But there are some varieties with other attributes that make them a more than worthwhile addition to any garden. *Prunus serrula* (Tibetan cherry) is a lovely, spring sight laden with small, white flowers mixed with fresh green foliage in late spring, but its real year-round attraction is the bark – deep mahogany-red with a satiny sheen that makes it irresistible to touch and stroke. To get the maximum benefit it's best planted where the sun shines on the bark, especially in winter. Height 3.9 m (13 feet). P. 'Amanogawa' (Lombardy cherry) is a narrow, columnar tree excellent in a confined space. Profuse quantities of shell-pink, semi-double flowers are borne in dense clusters from mid- to late spring. Its green leaves colour attractively in autumn. Height 3 m (10 feet). P. 'Pandora' is one of the earliest cherries to flower and is more delicately coloured than many other varieties. The ascending branches carry a mass of pale pink blossom in early and mid-spring, and this variety also gives good autumn leaf colour. Height 3.6 m (12 feet).

P. *subhirtella* 'Autumnalis Rosea' (autumn cherry) is quite different from its showy, spring cousins and is a delight to brighten the winter months. Its pale blush-pink flowers first appear in mid- to late autumn and continue right through to mid-spring. This variety does best in a sheltered site protected from winter winds. Plant it where it can be viewed from a window, so that the flowers can be appreciated to the full. A few sprigs of flowers cut when in bud make a lovely, indoor decoration. Because the flowers are over by spring, the autumn cherry is a good candidate for pairing with a summer-flowering climber such as the pearly white *Clematis* 'Marie Boisselot'. Height 3.6 m (12 feet).

Although the majority of trees flower during the spring, *Laburnum* × *watereri* 'Vossii' (golden rain tree) saves its show of glory until early summer, when the branches appear to be absolutely dripping with bright yellow racemes of flowers up to 60 cm (2 feet) long. All parts of the laburnum are poisonous, so it's not advisable to plant it where there are young children. The ferny, light green foliage is pleasant, but as laburnum has no other real ornamental features apart from its flowers I wouldn't recommend one if you are restricted to just one tree in your garden. Height 4.2 m (14 feet).

TREES FOR FRUITS OR BERRIES

All fruiting trees have at least two seasons of interest; their spring flowers, then their autumn fruits or berries. Many are also excellent for attracting wildlife into the garden in autumn and winter; birds such as migrating flocks of fieldfares and redwings arrive *en masse* in Britain to feed in autumn as well as resident birds such as blackbirds and thrushes. Birds have a distinct preference for red and orange berries; they leave white, pink and yellow fruits until much later or sometimes, in mild winters, do not eat them at all.

When siting a fruiting tree there are several points to bear in mind. It is best planted in a border and should be seen from the house so that its beauty can be admired to the full as the days get shorter and colder. Remember fruits eventually fall to the ground, so avoid the tree overhanging frequently used pathways, where fruit will be trodden into a mush and make the path dangerously slippery. Also do not plant trees bearing larger fruits in lawns, where fallen fruit can become a nuisance to the mower.

Cotoneasters bear heavy crops of orange or red berries in autumn and these are almost guaranteed to attract birds. These superb wildlife trees also produce white, spring flowers, which are popular with bees. *Cotoneaster* × *watereri* carries orange-red berries, and often retains most of its slender leaves through the winter. Height 4.2 m (14 feet).

Many *Malus* (crab apple) trees produce particularly good crops of fruit, which is both edible and ornamental. Flowers in mid-

to late spring are followed by fruits in autumn. M. 'John Downie' is the best variety for making delicious crab-apple jelly; it carries masses of white flowers and heavy crops of large, yellow-and-orange fruits. M. 'Golden Hornet' is a real autumn and winter

The branches of *Malus* 'Golden Hornet' (crab apple tree) are bowed under heavy crops of fruit in autumn, which often remain on the tree for months. In spring the tree is laden with white blossom.

brightener: its white flowers are followed by glowing, yellow fruits, which stay on the tree until well into winter. Two other varieties also holding fruit for a long time are M. 'Crittenden', with pale pink flowers and bright scarlet fruits, and M. 'Red Sentinel', with white flowers followed by large clusters of deep red fruits – these sometimes remain on the tree right through winter.

Sorbus cashmiriana – one of the very best small garden trees, bearing bunches of gleaming white berries from early autumn into winter.

Height 4.5 m (15 feet). An unusual variety is M. *toringoides*, an elegant, wide-spreading tree which blooms in late spring – slightly later than other varieties. Its flowers are creamy white and slightly fragrant. In autumn conspicuous, red-and-yellow, pear-shaped fruits make a wonderful display, and as an extra bonus the lobed leaves develop attractive autumn tints. Height 3 m (10 feet).

Sorbus are real winners for the small garden, with colourful crops of autumn berries as well as spring flowers, attractive leaf shapes and colourful autumn foliage. *Sorbus cashmiriana* (Kashmir sorbus) is a particular favourite. Most sorbus flowers are white, but this variety has delicate, blush-pink blooms borne in large, dense clusters in late spring, surrounded by feathery, fern-like foliage. Although the leaves often turn russet and gold in autumn, the marble-sized fruits are its outstanding glory; pearly white and hanging in clusters from the naked branches well into winter, they look like ethereal, white blossoms from a distance. Kashmir sorbus forms an open head of branches, and dislikes very dry soils. Height 3.6 m (12 feet).

Most forms of S. *aucuparia* (mountain ash or rowan) grow a little too large for the small garden. *S.a.* 'Fastigiata', however, is slow growing and ideal for the tiniest garden, forming a dense, upright column of branches clothed with fern-like foliage and bearing large bunches of glowing, red, autumn fruits. Height 2.4 m (8 feet). One of the best varieties for autumn colour is S. 'Embley', which carries heavy crops of bright orange-red fruits at the same time as the leaves turn rich scarlet, making a really fiery display. Height 3.9 m (13 feet). Yellow fruiting varieties provide a tremendous splash of cheerful colour. The aptly named S. 'Sunshine' bears large, dense clusters of bright golden-yellow fruits in autumn and is wonderful for offsetting the gloom of approaching winter. Its fern-like, green foliage often displays attractive, autumn tints as a backdrop to the fruits. It forms an erect head of branches. Height 3.9 m (13 feet).

As malus (crab apples) and sorbus form fairly open heads of branches, they allow plenty of light to filter through to the border underneath, so they can be underplanted with a wide range of plants that like partial shade. Shrubs such as hydrangeas, potentillas and philadelphus provide excellent summer colour, and evergreens such as *Viburnum tinus*, *V. davidii* and mahonias provide good winter interest.

WEEPING TREES

Weeping trees are perfect for small spaces, being usually grafted on top of a stem around 1.8 m (6 feet) high. They therefore tend not to grow much higher but simply build up a larger head of weeping branches – ideal if you want a tree but don't wish to overshadow any nearby windows. Most weeping trees make excellent specimens to place in a lawn or in a border underplanted with a carpet of prostrate plants such as cotoneaster, *Alchemilla mollis* or periwinkle. This enables the attractive shape to be fully appreciated.

Caraganas are excellent to give a splash of

sunshine to a 'Mediterranean' garden. They prefer dry soils but tolerate all except clay or wet soils. *Caragana arborescens* 'Pendula' (Siberian pea tree) forms a narrow umbrella of pendulous branches, which are covered in attractive pinnate leaves, and small, bright yellow flowers in early summer. *C.a.* 'Lorbergii' is similar but with almost needle-like leaves. Spread 1–1.2 m (3–4 feet).

Malus 'Royal Beauty' produces purplish-red stems falling in hanging cascades, covered with leaves of the same shade when young and turning dark green as they mature. The flowers and crab-apple fruit are a glowing dark red. Spread 1.2 m (4 feet).

Cherries are real harbingers of spring, and weeping cherries underplanted with a show of daffodils or tulips create a charming, spring picture. All too often, unfortunately, the weeping cherry most frequently sold in garden centres is *Prunus* 'Cheal's Weeping', which bears its rather garish double, pink flowers for only a short time and is somewhat dull for the rest of the year. Other weeping cherries, however, have a more attractive shape and slightly longer-lasting flowers. *P.* × *yedoensis* 'Shidare-yoshino' (Yoshino cherries) are graceful trees with arching branches falling in curtains to the ground. In early to mid-spring this breathtaking variety is wreathed in a profusion of delicately scented, blush-pink flowers. Even lovelier is *P.* × *y.* 'Ivensii', which makes a sheer waterfall of fragrant, pure white blossom. Spread 2.4 m (8 feet).

If width is no object, then the wide-spreading *P.* 'Pendula Rosea' (weeping spring cherry) is an absolute beauty to have in the garden. Its drooping branches form a wide canopy which in early to mid-spring are clothed in a cascade of pale pink blossom. Height varies depending on how the tree has been trained, but is usually around 2.4 m (8 feet). Spread 3–3.6 m (10–12 feet).

Willows have a bad press in relation to small gardens mainly owing to the widely planted weeping willow *Salix* × *chrysocoma*, whose roots may wreak havoc on drains and foundations if not planted at least 10 m (33 feet) from the house. The two weeping willows described here, however, can be safely planted in a small garden. My favourite is *S. purpurea* 'Pendula' (weeping purple willow) with its slender, reddish-purple branches falling gracefully to the ground, covered in delicate catkins in early spring and followed by slim, pointed leaves. If planted in a lawn it can act as a natural playhouse for young children. Rather more coarse in leaf but popular for its catkins is *S. caprea* 'Pendula' (Kilmarnock willow), a relative of pussy willow. The silver, furry catkins begin to appear in late winter and stay in their full glory for several weeks, turning yellow with pollen as spring advances. Willows associate well with water and both these trees look lovely next to a pond. They do well on a range of soils including boggy ground, but dislike very dry soils.

FRUIT TREES

There's nothing quite like the taste of fruit fresh-picked from your own garden, especially when you can be secure in the knowledge that no noxious chemicals have been used in its production. Fruit trees grown on dwarfing rootstocks are suitable for the small garden, though as they have only a short period of flower and fruit their ornamental value is rather limited.

There are plenty of ways of growing fruit in a small garden besides the traditional tree form. However small the ground space, almost every garden has fences or walls, and, so long as these receive a reasonable amount of sun, they provide an excellent site for growing trained fruit trees. These may be purchased ready-trained from the garden centre as espaliers or fans, but they tend to be expensive because of the initial, time-consuming pruning and training. If you have time and a little skill, it may be worth obtaining maiden (1-year-old) trees from a specialist fruit grower and training them yourself – young fruit trees can be trained not only against fences but also over arches and into goblet shapes.

With the majority of fruit trees you'll need at least two varieties to pollinate each other. At garden centres, apples and pears in particular are often divided into pollination groups indicating their flowering times. This can look confusing, but basically you need to choose trees either from the same group or from the adjacent groups, so they'll flower at the same time and pollinate each other. If you only have room for one apple tree, it's worth remembering that ornamental crab apples will pollinate ordinary apples.

Many varieties of plum, including 'Victoria', and also some cherries are self-fertile, which means they set a crop with their own pollen so no other tree is required. The same applies to peaches and nectarines, although these are more difficult to grow, needing a very sheltered, sunny site to crop successfully.

'Ballerina' columnar apple trees are tailor-made for the small garden. Given sufficient care, they can even be grown as patio plants in large tubs. Four of the Ballerinas are eating apples. 'Bolero' bears green fruit flushed with gold that has a crisp sharp flavour, and crops in early autumn. 'Flamenco' produces dark red fruit with a crisp tangy flavour in mid- to late-autumn, which stores well. 'Polka' bears bright red and green fruit with an excellent flavour, sweet and tangy, in early to mid-autumn. 'Waltz' bears dark red and green fruit in mid- to late-autumn, which is sweet and juicy, and also stores well.

'Charlotte' is the only cooking variety, and bears large green fruit flushed with red in mid-autumn – the fruit can be stored until well into the New Year. Malus 'Maypole' is a crab apple that produces bright pink flowers in spring, followed by large reddish-purple fruits in early autumn. Height 2.5 m (8 feet).

4

SHRUBS

Shrubs are the real backbone of a garden, which build up a framework of increasing ornamental value over the years. They provide a wealth of colour and interest right through the year with flowers, fruit, foliage or bark, as well as acting as a backdrop to enhance other plants. Most shrubs need little maintenance; and some are prostrate, ground-covering varieties that help suppress weeds.

There's a huge variety of shrubs available in many colours, shapes and sizes, so choosing the right ones for your garden can be no mean task. Size is the first consideration; many such as forsythia and deutzia grow far too big and have very limited periods of interest, but such quick-growing shrubs are often the cheapest on offer. Although the chance to save money can be tempting, do bear in mind that, because shrubs are long-lived and real value for money, a little extra expenditure on more worthwhile plants will make your garden much more attractive in the long term.

Aspect is most important when choosing shrubs, so in this chapter plants have been separated according to their preferences for full sun, sun/part shade or shade. Inevitably some plants fall into more than one category: berberis, cotoneaster and euonymus, for example, have been listed in the shady section, but are equally happy in part shade or full sun. Within each category shrubs have been separated according to whether their prime feature is flowers or foliage. There is also a separate section for lime-hating shrubs such as rhododendrons and azaleas that must have an acid soil. All sizes given are those reached after approximately 10 years.

SHRUBS FOR FULL SUN

Many sun-loving shrubs are at their peak in summer when they give a lavish display of colourful flowers. Fragrance adds an extra

Shrubs not only look superb in their own right, but also provide a backcloth to other plants. Red, mauve and pink rhododendrons are in flower; a skimmia forms a rounded dark green hummock, which makes a year-round contribution to the border.

dimension – many have aromatic leaves or fragrant flowers that release delicious wafts of scent on warm days, intensifying towards dusk or after a shower of rain. On a more prosaic note, it's worth including a good proportion of shrubs with attractive foliage, which give a border year-round interest as well as helping to enhance the flowers.

SHRUBS FOR FLOWERS

Throughout summer and autumn abelias produce masses of small, tubular flowers, which are displayed well against their attractive, glossy foliage; the gold-edged leaves of *Abelia* × *grandiflora* 'Francis Mason' are particularly pretty. Both this variety and *A.* × *grandiflora* have white flowers flushed with pink. *A.* 'Edward Goucher' bears lilac-pink flowers and bronze, young foliage, which matures to bright green. Abelias form rounded shrubs with gently arching branches, retain most of their foliage in winter, and do best in a sheltered site. Height and spread 1–1.2 m (3–4 feet).

Blue flowers look marvellous in a sunny border to provide striking colour. *Caryopteris* × *clandonensis* is splendid in late summer, bearing so many clusters of spiky, deep blue flowers that it appears to be a complete haze of blue – the aptly-named *C.* × *c.* 'Heavenly Blue' being one of the best cultivars. The small, aromatic, grey-green leaves are a perfect foil for the flowers, which are also attractive to bees.

Caryopteris does well on dry soils and looks good associated with yellow flowers: potentillas or *Clematis tangutica*, for example, or the annual climber *Tropaeolum peregrinum* (canary creeper) which can be threaded through an established caryopteris. Height 1–1.2 m (3–4 feet), spread 60 cm (2 feet).

Another blue-flowering shrub liking dry soils is *Ceratostigma willmottianum* (hardy plumbago) which produces rich cobalt-blue flowers from mid-summer to mid-autumn. Its leaves also develop attractive red tints in the autumn. It sometimes dies back to ground level in winter, and in spring dead stems should be pruned back to the new growth. Height 1 m (3 feet), spread 60 cm (2 feet).

Clusters of deliciously scented, white, pink-tinged flowers appear in late spring and again in summer on *Choisya* 'Aztec Pearl' – a new variety related to the popular *C. ternata* (Mexican orange blossom). It looks good all year, forming a neat, rounded bush of aromatic, evergreen leaves divided into slender glossy green leaflets. *C. ternata* 'Sundance' has golden foliage. It also bears white flowers in summer, although not as profuse or as scented as other varieties. This variety needs careful placing – full sun is best to bring out its golden colouring but can scorch young shoots. I find the best compromise is to grow it in light shade and settle for bright greeny-gold foliage. Height of both varieties 1.2 m (4 feet), spread 1 m (3 feet).

Few shrubs are more evocative of Mediterranean holidays than *Cistus* (sun rose) with its fragile, saucer-shaped flowers borne in early to mid-summer. The flowers are individually short-lived but produced in such quantity and succession as to give a continuous display. The aromatic, slightly sticky foliage is evergreen and either dark green or grey-green, depending on the variety. Most varieties are suited to the small garden and carry either white, pink or purple flowers. Several such as *C.* × *loretii* and *C.* × *dansereaui* are particularly handsome, with crimson, basal blotches on their large, white, papery petals. *C. crispus* has purplish-pink flowers and *C.* 'Silver Pink' produces silvery pale pink flowers, which go perfectly with its sage-green foliage. Sun rose flourishes in dry, impoverished soil and also does well on chalk; it may suffer frost damage in severe winters, so plant it near a wall for added protection. Height and spread 0.6–1.2 m (2–4 feet).

Closely related to *Cistus* – and also called sun roses – are × *Halimiocistus sahucii* and × *H.* 'Ingwersenii', which have narrow, dark green leaves and masses of small, pure white flowers in summer. They have a similar preference for dry conditions and their spreading habit makes a good contrast to rounded shrubs. Height and spread 30 cm (1 foot), spread 60 cm (2 feet).

Convolvulus cneorum has a delicate, understated beauty that makes it an essential plant for the border, especially one that is warm and sheltered with light soil. It forms a lax mound of satin-textured, silvery leaves and bears many white, pink-tinged, trumpet-shaped flowers in early summer. Height and spread 45 cm (18 inches.)

Another excellent though lesser-known silvery shrub is *Dorycnium hirsutum*, which boasts delightful, tiny, silver-grey leaves. Clusters of white, pink-tinged flowers borne at the ends of the stems in late summer are followed by reddish seed pods, which contrast well with the foliage. It has a loose, spreading habit and looks good tumbling over the edge of a path or at the base of a wall. Height and spread 60 cm (2 feet).

Cheerful splashes of gold can be provided in a small garden by the dwarf genistas, which are smothered in bright golden-yellow flowers in late spring and early summer. All are easily grown shrubs that love dry soils. *Genista lydia* is an outstanding plant forming a small mound of gently weeping stems smothered in golden-yellow flowers. Height and spread 30 cm (1 foot). Plant it so that it trails over the edge of a raised bed or rockery. Grow the prostrate varieties *G. pilosa* 'Lemon Spreader' and *G.p.* 'Vancouver Gold' in a similar position. Spread 60 cm (2 feet). *G. hispanica* (Spanish gorse) flourishes even on very dry soils, forming a dense mound of prickly foliage covered with golden flowers – it looks wonderful paired with rosemary. Height and spread 60 cm (2 feet).

Hebes are outstanding evergreen shrubs covered in small, dense flower spikes in summer. All hebes also thrive in seaside areas and all but the large-leaved and variegated varieties are usually hardy in severe winters. The many good varieties include *Hebe* 'Autumn Glory' with deep violet-blue flowers in late summer and autumn, *H.* × *franciscana* 'Blue Gem' with short racemes of bright blue flowers, and *H.* 'Great Orme', which has long, bright pink flowers. *H.* 'Mrs Winder' bears purplish foliage and blue flowers, while *H.* 'Youngii' (also known as *H.* 'Carl Teschner') is an excellent, low-growing variety with violet-and-white flowers. Promising newer varieties include *H.* 'Margret', which forms a low mound covered with sky-blue flowers, and *H.* 'Rosie', which has bright rosy pink flowers that pale a little with age. Most hebes are native to New Zealand and so look very much at home planted with *Phormium* (New Zealand flax). The smaller hebes such as *H.* 'Youngii' and *H.* 'Margret' look good edging borders and raised beds, and also associate well with dwarf conifers and alpines. Larger hebes such as *H.* 'Great Orme' contrast well with spiky-leaved plants such as irises and crocosmias. Height and spread 0.3–1 m (1–3 feet). More hebes are described in the following section on shrubs for foliage.

Parahebes are long-flowering dwarf shrubs related to hebes, which deserve to be grown more widely as their spreading habit makes them good ground cover and edging plants. Stems of tiny flowers are produced for months through late spring and summer – *Parahebe catarractae* bearing lilac-purple flowers and *P.* 'Miss Willmott' displaying glistening white flowers lightly veined with mauve. Height and spread 30 cm (1 foot).

Lavenders are popular with bees and butterflies, excellent for border edges and low hedges, and associate especially well with older houses and stonework. They are also an absolute must for the fragrant garden with their deliciously aromatic leaves and summer flower spikes in pink, white or blue – the blues being by far and away the most handsome. *Lavandula angustifolia* 'Hidcote' has deep violet-blue flowers, while *L.* 'Munstead' and *L.* 'Twickel Purple' carry flowers of lavender-blue. Height and spread 60 cm (2 feet). *L.* 'Vera' (Dutch lavender) and *L.* 'Grappenhall' also produce lavender-blue flowers and just have the edge for scent – they're also a little taller, at 0.6–1 m (2–3 feet). *L. stoechas* (French lavender) is a lovely, aromatic plant for a sheltered site, bearing masses of unusual, dark purple flowers topped with a pair of wing-like bracts in summer. *L.s.* subsp. *pedunculata* (Spanish lavender), which is often named *L.* 'Papillon', has shorter flower spikes and appears to be slightly hardier than *L.*

Lavandula stoechas (French lavender) with its unusual purple flowers, associates well with the silvery foliage of *Santolina* in this sunny border. The large seedheads belong to the ornamental onion *Allium christophii*.

stoechas. Height 60 cm (2 feet), spread 45 cm (18 inches).

Perovskia atriplicifolia 'Blue Spire' (Russian sage) blooms in late summer, bearing tall, open spires of lavender-blue flowers. These are set off perfectly by small, toothed, grey-green leaves, which give off a pungent, sage-like smell when crushed. The slender, white stems look good in winter, especially when Russian sage is planted in groups of three. Cut the stems hard back in spring to encourage new growth. Height 1 m (3 feet), spread 45 cm (18 inches).

Phygelius is an exotic-looking and unusual semi-evergreen shrub bearing tall stems of many tubular flowers in shades of yellow, red or pink in summer and autumn. It does best in a sheltered position; if grown with its back to a wall it may reach 1.5 m (5 feet), but elsewhere reaches around 1 m (3 feet) with a spread of 60 cm (2 feet). Cut back hard in spring to maintain a bushy shape. Good varieties include *Phygelius capensis* 'Coccineus' with deep orange-red flowers, *P. aequalis* 'Yellow Trumpet' with large, creamy yellow flowers, and *P. × rectus* 'Pink Elf' has pale pink, crimson-edged flowers.

For sheer elegance *Romneya coulteri* (tree poppy) is hard to beat. In summer and autumn it bears huge flowers, with crinkly, white petals and a central boss of golden stamens, on top of tall, slender stems covered in attractively divided, glaucous leaves. Tree poppies are best cut back to within around 5

Shades of blue – *Nepeta mussinii* (catmint) in the foreground and behind, the tall blue flowers of *Perovskia* (Russian sage) tone well with the coloured foliage of *Salvia* 'Purpurascens' (purple sage).

cm (2 inches) of the ground in mid-spring; they often die back to ground level in cold winters. If they really like your garden, tree poppies may be invasive. Height 1.2–1.5 m (4–5 feet), spread 1 m (3 feet).

The dense, spiky, evergreen foliage of *Rosmarinus officinalis* (rosemary) provides all-year interest and an immensely useful, dark green background to other plants, as well as bearing hundreds of tiny, blue flowers all along its stems in late spring. It also boasts numerous culinary uses, too, and does well on dry soil. The best variety is *R.o.* 'Miss Jessop's Upright', which has a tall, narrow habit. Height 1.5 m (5 feet), spread 1 m (3 feet).

Many heads of button-like flowers appear in mid-summer on *Santolina* (cotton lavender) – a useful plant forming a low mound of evergreen woolly foliage. *S. chamaecyparissus* (also known as *S. incana*) has dense, grey foliage and bright yellow flowers, and makes an excellent low hedge – it looks especially good when edging a herb garden. I find *S. pinnata* subsp. *neapolitana* is a more attractive border plant, with its feathery, silver foliage and slightly paler yellow flowers. *S. rosmarinifolia* has vivid green, thread-like foliage and bright yellow flowers; *S.r.* 'Primrose Gem' carries softer yellow flowers. Santolinas are best clipped hard in spring to maintain a neat mound of foliage. Height and spread 45 cm (18 inches).

SHRUBS FOR FOLIAGE

Foliage plants are invaluable in any border, but especially so in a sunny site where too many bright flower colours can become a little overwhelming at times. Grey- and silver-foliaged plants in particular revel in hot, dry conditions and are lovely to 'weave' through a border, both cooling and accentuating brighter flowers and foliage.

Best of all silver-foliaged plants is *Artemisia* 'Powis Castle', which spreads its filigree foliage in lacy cushions and is marvellous at softening the edges of paths or paving. It makes an excellent companion to virtually everything, and looks superb with blue-flowered and purple-leaved plants. Height and spread 60 cm (2 feet).

Several hebes possess very attractive foliage. Almost indispensable is *Hebe pinguifolia* 'Pagei', a spreading variety forming frosty mats of small, glaucous leaves – good for edging borders or raised beds and an excellent foil for brightly coloured flowers. White flowers in summer are a bonus. Height 15 cm (6 inches), spread 45 cm (18 inches). Slightly bushier is *H. pimeleoides* 'Quicksilver', which has minute, silvery blue leaves and pale lilac flowers in summer. *H.* 'Red Edge' forms a compact mound of blue-grey leaves margined with red – in winter, when the red tints deepen, it looks especially effective. Height and spread 45 cm (18 inches).

The strong curry smell of *Helichrysum italicum* subsp. *serotinum* (curry plant) can be almost overpowering at times – people tend to love it or loathe it. Neat mounds of narrow, intense silver-grey leaves are topped with masses of bright yellow, button-like flowers in summer. Plant it next to a path, so that, it releases the scent as you brush against it. Height and spread 60 cm (2 feet).

Spiky foliage breaks up the rounded shapes that often prevail in a border, and one of the most striking, spiky leaved plants is *Phormium* (New Zealand flax) with its bold

FRAGRANT PLANTS

Many marvellous plants possess fragrant flowers or aromatic foliage, and just a few can greatly enhance the enjoyment of a garden. The scent of plants can be as important as their looks, and fragrant plants are among my most beloved garden residents – their perfume greets the casual stroller round the garden and wafts gently through the air on soft, summer evenings.

Anyone with poor sight will particularly treasure the many and varied fragrances a garden can offer.

Carpets of thyme with their aromatic flowers and foliage edge the paths of this rose garden. Many herbs such as thyme are fragrant, but not all roses are scented – it's well worth selecting the most perfumed varieties.

SCENTED FLOWERS

Aponogeton distachyos (water hawthorn) (see page 122)

Camellia 'Narumi-gata' (see page 56)

Choisya (orange blossom) (see page 34)

Clematis heracleifolia and *C. armandii* (see pages 86 and 76)

Cosmos atrosanguineus (chocolate plant) (see page 119)

Daphne (see pages 43–4)

Dianthus (see page 90)

Fothergilla gardenii (see page 56)

Hesperis matronalis (dame's violet or sweet rocket) (see page 118)

Jasminum (see page 74)

Laburnum (golden rain tree) (see page 26)

Lathyrus odoratus (sweet pea) (see page 118)

Lavandula (see page 36)

Lonicera (honeysuckle) (see page 74)

Mahonia (see page 50)

Malus coronaria 'Charlottae' and *M. floribunda* (see page 23)

Matthiola bicornis (night-scented stock) (see page 112)

Nicotiana (tobacco plant) (see page 112)

Perovskia atriplicifolia 'Blue Spire' (Russian sage) (see page 38)

Philadelphus (mock orange) (see page 45)

Phlox paniculata (see page 94)

Pieris (see page 56)

Primula florindae and *P. sikkimensis* (see page 125)

Prunus × *yedoensis* (Yoshino cherry) (see page 30)

Reseda odorata (mignonette) (see page 112)

Romneya coulteri (tree poppy) (see page 38)

Roses (many varieties) (see pages 58–63)

Sarcococca (Christmas box) (see page 50)

Skimmias, especially *S. japonica* 'Rubella' (see page 51)

Trachelospermum (see page 77)

Viburnum × *juddii* (see page 46)

Wisteria (see pages 74–5)

AROMATIC FOLIAGE

Artemisia (see pages 39 and 108)

Caryopteris (see page 34)

Cistus (sun rose) (see page 35)

Helichrysum italicum subsp. *serotinum* (curry plant) (see page 39)

Houttuynia cordata 'Chamaeleon' (see pages 124–5)

Lavandula (see page 36)

Nepeta (catmint) (see page 90)

Origanum vulgare 'Aureum' (golden marjoram) (see page 91)

Perovskia atriplicifolia 'Blue Spire' (Russian sage) (see page 38)

Rosmarinus (see page 38)

Ruta graveolens (rue) (see page 43)

Salvia (sage) (see page 43)

Santolina (cotton lavender) (see page 39)

This enchanting little statue is surrounded by a subtle group of plants. *Ruta graveolens* (rue) has beautifully-shaped intense blue leaves, and goes well with the ferny foliage and white flowers of a *Potentilla*. Higher up sprays of variegated *Euonymus* leaves give colour all year.

clumps of long, sword-like leaves. Varieties with plain green or purple leaves are the most vigorous; those with coloured or variegated leaves tend to be less vigorous and more compact. These include P. 'Dazzler' which has dark purple leaves striped warm red in the centre, P. 'Maori Sunrise' produces pinkish leaves edged with bronze-red, and P. 'Cream Delight' has leaves elegantly striped with cream and green. New Zealand flax prefers a good, moisture-retentive soil. It may suffer frost damage in a severe winter; a good safeguard is to grow it in a tub for an exotic patio display, and bring it into a greenhouse or conservatory in winter. Height 1 m (3 feet), spread 60 cm (2 feet).

The intense, glaucous blue, evergreen foliage of *Ruta graveolens* 'Jackman's Blue' (rue) is very ornamental and makes a good contrast to silver- or purple leaved plants. In summer it bears clusters of tiny, mustard-yellow flowers. Avoid smelling the crushed leaves if you can, however: they have the most appalling smell! Rue produces an allergic skin reaction in some people, so wear gloves when dealing with it. Height and spread 45 cm (18 inches).

Varieties of *Salvia officinalis* (sage) with coloured foliage are good plants for both ornamental and culinary uses. The two best varieties are *S.o.* 'Icterina', with leaves brightly variegated green and gold, and *S.o.* 'Purpurascens', which has leaves deeply flushed with purple. *S.o.* 'Tricolor', which produces pretty white, pink and purple foliage, is only reliably hardy in milder areas. These varieties of sage are particularly good to add colour to a herb garden as well as a border, and associate well with other herbs such as lavender, santolina, rosemary and rue. Height and spread 45 cm (18 inches).

Yuccas originate from the American desert regions and only flourish in sunny, dry situations. They form rosettes of narrow, rigid leaves, and those with coloured foliage are most ornamental. *Yucca filamentosa* 'Bright Edge' has leaves margined bright yellow while *Y. flaccida* 'Golden Sword' produces green leaves with a bold, central stripe of creamy yellow. Height and spread 60 cm (2 feet).

SHRUBS FOR SUN/PART SHADE

The plants in this section generally do best in part shade, although, with a few exceptions, they will also grow in full sun provided they have a good, moisture-retentive soil.

SHRUBS FOR FLOWERS

Daphnes are choice plants – amongst the loveliest of all shrubs – bearing many delicate and beautiful clusters of exceptionally fragrant, long-lasting flowers. They can be hard to establish and many species are exacting in their requirements, needing a well-prepared, loamy moisture-retentive soil with good drainage.

Daphne × *burkwoodii* is one of the easiest to grow. It forms an upright, slightly rounded bush and tends to lose its leaves in only hard winters. In late spring and early summer, and again in autumn, it carries many clusters of pale pink flowers. Height 1 m (3 feet), spread 60 cm (2 feet). *D. mezereum* (mezereon) is a colourful, old-fashioned plant with purplish-red flowers clustered all along its naked branches in late winter and early spring, followed by glistening, scarlet berries in summer. *D.m.* 'Alba' is a white-flowering variety with amber-yellow berries, which – like all mezereon berries – are poisonous. Unlike many daphnes, *D. mezereum* does well on chalky soils. Height 1–1.2 m (3–4 feet), spread 60 cm (2 feet).

D. odora 'Aureomarginata' is a real herald of spring; from late winter to late spring it produces many clusters of reddish-purple flowers, paling with age, which have a strong and delicious fragrance. It forms a loose dome of glossy, evergreen leaves narrowly margined with creamy yellow. Height and spread 1–1.2 m (3–4 feet). *D. × napolitana* is also evergreen but with tiny, mid-green leaves, bearing small clusters of rose-pink flowers through spring to early summer. It's a dainty, little shrub suitable for a tub or rock garden. Height and spread 60 cm (2 feet).

The showy, dangling flowers of fuchsias are superb for providing a wealth of colour from summer right through autumn. Only hardy varieties are covered here, but there are also numerous half-hardy fuchsias available, which are popular for tubs and hanging baskets. In severe winters, protect fuchsia bases with straw or bracken. The branches give added frost protection, so fuchsias shouldn't be pruned until spring, when all stems can be removed almost to ground level. Good hardy varieties include *Fuchsia* 'Alice Hoffman' and *F.* 'Lady Thumb' with red and white flowers; and *F.* 'Mrs Popple' and *F.* 'Tom Thumb' with scarlet and violet flowers. *F.* 'Genii' has golden foliage turning lime-yellow in summer, contrasting well with violet and red flowers. *F. magellanica* 'Versicolor' is a tough variety, its leaves – variegated pale green, cream and white – going very well with the small, red flowers.

Daphne odora 'Aureomarginata' – one of the best shrubs for early spring colour and fragrance. The exquisitely-scented flowers last for months.

Height and spread 60 cm–1.2 m (2–4 feet).

Hydrangeas are invaluable, summer-flowering shrubs with striking, showy flower heads borne from mid-summer to early autumn. They do best on a rich, slightly acid soil that isn't too dry in summer, and go well with the handsome foliage of hardy ferns. Their exact flower colour depends on whether the soil is acid or limy. One of the best species for the small garden is *Hydrangea serrata* with flat, lacecap-type flowers. *H.s.* 'Bluebird' displays lovely, deep sea-blue flowers – the outer florets turning reddish-mauve on limy soils. *H.s.* 'Grayswood' has blue flowers edged by a ring of white florets that change gradually to deep red. *H.s.*

'Preziosa' boasts handsome, purplish stems and purple-tinged leaves, topped with heads of deep rose-pink flowers. Height and spread 1–1.2 m (3–4 feet).

H. macrophylla produces eye-catching 'mop-heads' of flowers. Although most varieties grow too large, there are a few good, compact ones: H.m. 'Ami Pasquier' has dark red flowers, H.m. 'Miss Belgium' carries rosy red ones; and those on H.m. 'President Doumer' are dark wine-red on limy soil and dark blue or purple on acid soil. Height and spread 1 m (3 feet). Slow-growing H.m. 'Pia', with its deep purplish-red flowers, is also ideal for growing in a tub. Height and spread 60 cm (2 feet).

A popular and easily-grown, semi-evergreen shrub is Hypericum 'Hidcote', which produces golden, saucer-shaped flowers up to 8 cm (3 inches) across from mid-summer through to the end of autumn. It prefers a well-drained soil and is happy in full sun as well as partial shade. Height and spread 1.2 m (4 feet).

One of the true essences of mid-summer is the sweet scent of Philadelphus (mock orange blossom), beloved for its fragrant, white flowers. Several of the best, smaller varieties include P. 'Avalanche', P. 'Sybille', and P. microphyllus, which have single flowers, and P. 'Frosty Morn' and P. 'Manteau d'Hermine' which develop double flowers. This deciduous, twiggy, rounded shrub is easily grown in sun as well as partial shade and tolerates poor soils

including shallow chalk. It makes a perfect combination with English roses for an old-fashioned, floral display and a wealth of scent. Height 1–1.5 m (3–5 feet), spread 1 m (3 feet).

Also easy to grow and splendid for their long flowering season are potentillas, which produce masses of single flowers from late spring and often right through till autumn. They come in a wide range of flower colours: pink, orange and red flowers, however, tend to fade if sited in full sun. Most potentillas form rounded bushes covered with deciduous, ferny foliage. Potentilla 'Elizabeth' carries large, bright yellow flowers; P. 'Red Ace' produces orange-red ones; P. 'Red Robin' is a deeper version of the same shade; and P. 'Princess' bears pale pink flowers. P. 'Tangerine' bears flowers the same colour as its name. Height and spread 1 m (3 feet). Several potentillas such as P. 'Manchu' have a low, spreading habit. This variety produces white flowers and grey-green foliage. Height 45 cm (18 inches), spread 1 m (3 feet).

Spiraea japonica varieties bear many flat flower heads from mid-summer onwards and are easy, reliable, deciduous shrubs. S.j. 'Little Princess' has deep pink flowers, while those of S.j. 'Shirobana' are unusual – being a mixture of deep pink and white. For a really eye-catching colour, choose S.j. 'Anthony Waterer', with its bright crimson flowers. As well as interesting flowers, several varieties also have attractive golden foliage. *S.j.* 'Goldflame' produces reddish-orange leaves in early spring, which turn golden-yellow, making a sharp contrast to the bright carmine-pink flowers in summer. *S.j.* 'Gold Mound' is more subtle, with softer yellow foliage from spring to autumn and pale pink flowers. Height and spread of 60 cm (2 feet).

Viburnums are classic shrubs to give form and style to the garden, and some have deliciously scented flowers. Only a few are suitable for small gardens, but these alone give colour and interest in every season of the year. *Viburnum davidii* is a useful evergreen with glossy, leathery leaves that are deeply ridged and veined. Small clusters of white flowers are borne at the ends of the stems in early summer, and may be followed in autumn by small, egg-shaped berries of an eye-catching shade of turquoise-blue. Male and female plants are needed for pollination and berry production. As there's no reliable way of 'sexing' viburnum, planting a group of three increases the chances of successful pollination. This plant makes good ground cover, forming a low, spreading mound, and tolerates almost total shade as well as sun. Height 60 cm (2 feet), spread 1 m (3 feet).

One of my all-time favourites is *V.* × *juddii*, which is covered in large, white, pink-tinged flower heads, deliciously and almost overpoweringly scented, in mid- to late spring. It forms a rounded, deciduous bush that offers little interest apart from its flowers; it can, however, be brightened up by threading a summer-flowering clematis through its branches. Height and spread 1.2 m (4 feet).

Autumn is the season of glory for *V. opulus* 'Compactum' (guelder rose) which bears so many showy clusters of glistening, red berries that its branches are almost weighed down – its white flower heads having appeared in spring. This deciduous, neat, rounded bush grows well in all, including wet, soils. Height and spread 1 m (3 feet). *V. tinus* 'Eve Price' (laurustinus) is excellent for winter interest, both from its many flat heads of white, pink-tinged flowers borne from winter into spring and its dark evergreen foliage. It has a bushy, upright shape. Height 1.2 m (4 feet), spread 1 m (3 feet). *V.t.* 'Variegatum' bears leaves that are attractively variegated with creamy yellow; it is reliably hardy only in milder areas.

Weigelas are popular, deciduous shrubs. Most varieties grow very large but some recent introductions are said to be more compact: *Weigela florida* 'Minuet' bears reddish-purple, bell-like flowers in clusters against green foliage, which becomes tinged with purple in summer. *W.* 'Victoria' has deep rosy red flowers and dark purplish-green leaves. *W.* 'Tango' has bronze-purple leaves and dark red flowers. Height and spread 1–1.2 m (3–4 feet). An unusual species for the connoisseur is *W. middendorffiana*, with its delightful, sulphur-yellow, foxglove-like flowers, marked with dark orange in the throat, in mid- to late spring. The peeling bark provides winter interest. This plant does best in a sheltered, partially shaded site. Height and spread 1 m (3 feet).

SHRUBS FOR FOLIAGE

Acer palmatum (Japanese maple) varieties are among the most delicate and appealing of all foliage shrubs. The *A.p.* 'Dissectum' varieties form mushroom-shaped bushes

The delicate ferny foliage of *Acer palmatum* 'Dissectum' (Japanese maple) coupled with its mounded habit, makes it a perfect companion for water in the garden and helps this pond blend into the surrounding planting.

covered with leaves finely divided into seven or nine lobes. Even though they lose their leaves in winter, their elegant skeletons still look very stylish. Japanese maples make splendid feature plants for patios and town gardens in tubs or borders, and associate especially well with water. They are expensive, however, so buy only if you have the right conditions – a loamy, moist but well-drained, neutral or acid soil in a site sheltered from cold winds. Most popular is *A.p.* 'Dissectum' with its fresh green leaves. *A.p.* 'Dissectum Atropurpureum' has deep reddish-purple leaves, as does *A.p.* 'Inaba-shidare', which turns crimson in autumn. Height and spread 1 m (3 feet).

Berberis thunbergii varieties are easily grown shrubs in a wide range of attractive foliage colours. All are deciduous, with prickly stems and small, yellow flowers in spring, but foliage is definitely their main asset. Berberis flourish on all soils except boggy ground, and those with purple foliage associate very well with grey or silver foliage. *B.t.* 'Atropurpurea Nana' and *B.t.* 'Bagatelle' are two purple-leaved dwarfs, with a height and spread of 45 cm (18 inches). *B.t.* 'Aurea' has handsome, bright golden foliage in spring, tinged green by summer; avoid full sun which may scorch the delicate leaves. *B.t.* 'Green Carpet' produces fresh green leaves on arching stems while *B.t.* 'Kelleriis' has green leaves mottled with white, the white parts turning pink and red in autumn. Height and spread 60 cm–1 m (2–3 feet).

Several varieties possess arching stems with purple leaves attractively mottled silver-pink. *B.t.* 'Pink Queen' is the best, closely followed by *B.t.* 'Rose Glow' and *B.t.* 'Harlequin'. Height and spread 1–1.2 m (3–4 feet). For a real contrast of shape, *B.t.* 'Helmond Pillar' forms an upright column of dark purple foliage. Height 1 m (3 feet), spread 45 cm (18 inches). More berberis are described in the following section on shrubs for shade.

Cornus alba (dogwood) varieties are excellent for year-round interest; most have coloured or variegated foliage, and all varieties boast coloured stems for winter interest. Dogwoods generally produce better, more colourful stems if pruned back to 20 cm (8 inches) every spring (or alternate years on heavy clay soil); if left unpruned they get too large for the small garden. For several weeks the bare stumps reproach your severity, but by early summer you should have a flourishing mass of new shoots. Dogwoods are happy on soils ranging from dry to boggy. My favourite variety is *C.a.* 'Aurea' with its soft gold leaves, which make a superb backcloth to the blue flowers of plants such as iris and asters. The leaves of *C.a.* 'Spaethii' are brightly variegated green and gold, while those of *C.a.* 'Elegantissima' are green and white. *C. sanguinea* 'Winter Flame' is a new variety that brightens the dark half of the year. In autumn its soft green leaves turn an eye-catching orange and yellow; they then fall to

A purple-leaved berberis catches the eye in the centre of this mixed border, and its colour is echoed above by a dark red *Clematis viticella*, which rambles through the larger shrubs.

reveal fiery orange and red stems, which should be hard pruned in spring. Height (if pruned) 1.2 m (4 feet), spread 1 m (3 feet).

Golden-leaved evergreens really come into their own in winter, though of course they look good all year round. *Ilex crenata* 'Golden Gem' (Japanese holly) has tiny, gold leaves; it makes a good, low hedge and responds well to trimming. It's best to avoid siting it in full sun, which can scorch the leaves. Height 60 cm (2 feet), spread 1 m (3 feet).

Another pleasing, golden evergreen is

Lonicera nitida 'Baggesen's Gold' with its many sprays of tiny, yellow leaves. Again it responds well to clipping if used for a hedge, or makes a handsome shrub for the border. A light haircut in early spring keeps the foliage at its best; the leaves are most colourful from spring to autumn, and turn greenish-yellow in winter. Height 1.2 m (4 feet), spread 1 m (3 feet).

Dwarf *Salix* (willow) varieties are choice, little shrubs for borders and tubs, with attractive foliage and catkins. *S.* × *boydii* has greyish, felted leaves, a gnarled, ancient appearance and is suitable for the rock garden. Height and spread 45 cm (18 inches). *S. helvetica* carries silver-grey catkins in spring, at the same time as its grey-green leaves. *S. lanata* (woolly willow) boasts attractive silver-grey, hairy leaves and yellowish catkins in spring; this is one of the few grey-leaved shrubs that does equally well in sun or shade. Unlike most willows, these varieties dislike a boggy soil. Height and spread 1 m (3 feet).

Sambucus racemosa 'Tenuifolia' (cut-leaved elder) is sometimes called the 'poor man's Japanese maple', which sounds rather derogatory. It is, however, a very handsome plant that also tolerates a limy soil, which Japanese maples dislike. Unlike its rampant cousins of the elder family, this variety forms a low, weeping mound of fern-like, fresh green, deciduous foliage, which looks particularly lovely near water. Height and spread 1 m (3 feet).

SHRUBS FOR SHADE

Shrubs for shady sites need to be chosen with care as there are comparatively few that flourish away from the sun. Those that do, however, are mostly handsome plants with bold, glossy, evergreen foliage of different leaf shapes and textures, which combine to make an enduring and attractive picture that is an asset to any garden. These shrubs are particularly valuable in giving shape to town gardens shaded by high surrounding walls. All the shrubs in this section are also happy in part shade, though most dislike very sunny situations.

SHRUBS FOR FLOWERS AND BERRIES

Berberis are amongst the most tolerant and easily grown of all shrubs and flourish in all aspects. They come in a wide range of deciduous and evergreen varieties, most of which carry yellow flowers in spring and are well endowed with thorns. Colourful autumn berries are the main feature of several deciduous varieties: *Berberis* × *carminea* 'Bountiful' and *B.* × *c.* 'Pirate King' bear heavy crops of bright orange-red berries. *B.* 'Rubrostilla' is one of the most spectacular, producing heavy crops of large, glowing coral-red berries. Height 1.2 m (4 feet), spread 1 m (3 feet). Good evergreen varieties include *B. candidula*, which forms a dome-shaped bush of small, glossy leaves, and *B.* × *frikartii* 'Amstelveen', which is similar but with gently arching branches;

the leaves of both varieties are silvery underneath. *B. gagnepainii* has bluish-black berries in autumn and develops a dense bush of upright stems. Its prickly stems make a good barrier. Height 1.2 m (4 feet), spread 1 m (3 feet).

Cotoneasters carry white flowers in late spring followed by good autumn colour from leaves or berries. They are also very easy shrubs to grow and tolerant of all but the most extreme soils and situations. The best varieties for the small garden are evergreens for ground cover: *Cotoneaster congestus* forms a mounded, dense carpet of tiny, dark green leaves, but only bears a few berries, while *C. dammeri* has long, vigorous shoots covered with large, pointed leaves and bears bright red fruits. *C.* 'Gnom' develops a wide-spreading mound of arching shoots covered with pointed, dark green leaves that are tinged bronze in winter, and bears small red berries. *C. microphyllus* forms a wide mound of stiff branches with tiny leaves, and has reddish-pink berries. Height 15–60 cm (6 inches–2 feet), spread 1–1.2 m (3–4 feet).

Numerous small, yellow flowers appear from early summer to autumn on *Hypericum androsaemum*, followed by dark red fruits that eventually turn black. The rounded leaves on this mounded, deciduous shrub look good with a glossy green clump of *Iris foetidissima*. Height 1 m (3 feet), spread 60 cm (2 feet).

Mahonias are useful shrubs flowering in late winter and early spring, which also provide interest all year round with their bold, spiny, evergreen foliage. The majority are too large and vigorous for a small garden, though *Mahonia aquifolium* 'Smaragd' (Oregon grape) is fairly compact. It carries dark glossy green leaves that are attractively bronze-coloured when young and dense clusters of bright yellow flowers. Height 1–1.2 m (3–4 feet), spread 0.6–1 m (2–3 feet).

Marvellous for fragrant flowers is *Sarcococca* (Christmas box) – a greatly undervalued shrub that forms a neat clump of upright stems covered in glossy, pointed, evergreen leaves, and bears little tassels of creamy white flowers all along its stems from mid-winter to early spring. The flowers exude a strong, vanilla-like scent. For maximum appreciation this plant should be placed near a frequently used pathway or door; even better, grow it in a tub to bring indoors and scent a porch or conservatory. There are several excellent but similar species: *S. confusa*, *S. hookeriana* var. *digyna* and *S. humilis*. All prefer full or part shade in any reasonably fertile soil. Height 0.6–1 m (2–3 feet), spread 45–60 cm (18–24 inches).

Skimmias bear showy clusters of flower buds through winter, which open into starry, white flowers in mid- to late spring. These are followed by brightly coloured berries on female plants later in the year, but you do need to have plants of both sexes in order for the female plants to berry. These neat, evergreen shrubs have dark glossy leaves and a trim rounded shape, and look good all year. Skimmias prefer full or part shade on acid or neutral soils, though, with the exception of *Skimmia japonica* subsp. *reevesiana*, they will also tolerate more alkaline soils. If limy soil does cause chlorosis – when the leaves turn yellow, particularly between the veins – feed them with sequestered iron once or twice a year. One of the few hermaphrodite varieties (bearing male and female flowers on the same plant) is *S.j.* subsp. *reevesiana*. This compact shrub produces showy clusters of bright red berries, which last through winter and are often still there when the flowers open. Height and spread 60 cm (12 feet). Other good varieties include: *S.j.* 'Fragrans', a male form with panicles of fragrant, white flowers; *S.j.* 'Nymans', a female variety that bears heavy crops of red fruits, as does *S.j.* 'Foremanii' (also known as *S.j.* 'Veitchii'). *S.j.* 'Rubella' is a male variety with showy clusters of red flower buds through winter opening to white flowers in spring. Height 1–1.2 m (3–4 feet), spread 0.6–1 m (2–3 feet).

Vinca minor (lesser periwinkle) makes excellent ground cover and is good for underplanting shrubs and trees. It produces long, trailing shoots with glossy, evergreen leaves; the shoots root at intervals as they spread, eventually layering to form a solid carpet covered with bright blue flowers in spring and early summer. Lesser periwinkle is easily pleased, happy in conditions from full shade to full sun, and likes any reasonably fertile soil. *V.m.* 'Argenteovariegata' has green and white variegated leaves, while those of *V.m.* 'Aureovariegata' are splashed with gold. *V.m.* 'Azurea Flore Pleno' bears double, pale blue flowers. The sparkling white flowers of *V.m.* 'Gertrude Jekyll' are shown off to perfection against its dark green foliage. Periwinkles can also be used to trail over the edges of large tubs or even in hanging baskets for winter colour. Bulbs planted amongst their carpets of foliage make a lovely display, and unsightly dying bulb foliage is neatly concealed too.

Avoid the rampant *Vinca major* (greater periwinkle) which is an absolute pest in a small garden and should be avoided like the plague unless you have a large area of waste ground to cover!

SHRUBS FOR FOLIAGE

Bamboos are graceful, elegant plants, forming neat, upright clumps of attractive, grassy leaves that rustle gently in the lightest breeze. They look especially good in tubs, surrounded by cobblestones, or planted near water. They're happy in full or light shade and prefer a good moisture-retentive soil, although they dislike waterlogged ground. *Arundinaria viridistriata* is a superb, coloured bamboo with leaves brightly striped yellow and green. Cutting the foliage back almost to the ground in autumn encourages good growth for the following year. *A. fortunei* (also known as *A.*

PLANTS FOR WINTER COLOUR

After the flaming displays of autumn colour, the cold, dark days of winter may seem interminable. But even in winter there are plants that bring colour to the garden. The fragile beauty of winter flowers would be vastly overshadowed at any other time of year, but in these darkest months they become treasured possessions that lift the spirits immeasurably. Plants with attractive bark also look colourful, as do fruit- and berry-bearing plants that hold their fruit well into winter – provided they are not eaten by wildlife. Although birds tend to prefer red or orange fruits, in a hard winter they devour anything edible. Numerous evergreen shrubs and conifers that aren't covered in detail here also take centre stage in winter, particularly those with golden or coloured foliage.

There are plants to provide lots of colour even in the depths of winter. The red stems of *Cornus* (dogwoods) provide a wonderful backdrop to the light green flowers and dark glossy foliage of *Helleborus foetidus*. In the foreground ivies and winter-flowering heathers add extra interest.

WINTER-FLOWERING PLANTS

Camellia sasanqua
(see page 56)

Clematis cirrhosa
(see page 76)

Daphne odora
'Aureomarginata'
(see page 44)

D. mezereum (mezereon)
(see page 43)

Erica carnea varieties
(winter heathers)
(see page 111)

Hebe 'Red Edge'
(see page 39)

Hellebores (see page 97)

Jasminum nudiflorum
(winter jasmine)
(see page 69)

Mahonia aquifolium
'Smaragd' (see page 50)

Prunus subhirtella
'Autumnalis Rosea'
(autumn cherry)
(see page 26)

Sarcococca (Christmas
box) (see page 50)

Schizostylis coccinea (Kaffir
lily) (see page 90)

Skimmia (see page 51)

Viburnum tinus 'Eve Price'
(laurustinus)
(see page 46)

PLANTS WITH ATTRACTIVE OR COLOURFUL BARK

Acer pensylvanicum and
Acer grosseri var. *hersii*
(snakebark maples)
(see page 21)

Cornus alba varieties
(dogwoods)
(see page 48)

C. sanguinea 'Winter Flame'
(see page 48)

Prunus serrula (Tibetan
cherry) (see page 26)

Weigela middendorffiana
(see page 46)

PLANTS WITH LONG-LASTING FRUIT OR BERRIES

Aucuba japonica 'Rozannie'
(see page 54)

Iris foetidissima (Gladwin
iris) (see page 98)

Malus 'Golden Hornet',
'Crittenden' and 'Red
Sentinel' (crab apples)
(see pages 27–8)

Skimmias, especially
reevesiana (see page 51)

Sorbus cashmiriana
(Kashmir sorbus)
(see page 29)

S. 'Sunshine' (see page 29)

Dwarf bamboo *Arundinaria viridistriata* is set off well by cobblestones, and contrasts with the pink hydrangea flowers and spiky shape of a variegated yucca.

variegata) produces leaves that are striped white and pale green. Height 1–1.2 m (3–4 feet), spread 60 cm (2 feet). Tall varieties of bamboo such as *A. rundinaria murieliae* grow to around 1.8 m (6 feet) and make good feature plants. *Shibataea kumasasa*, by contrast, is a compact bamboo. Broadbladed, fresh green leaves appear on green stems, which become brownish-green with age. *S. kumasasa* forms a dense clump and is particularly happy in a moist soil. Height and spread 60 cm (2 feet).

Aucuba japonica (spotted laurel) is a rounded shrub with large, glossy, evergreen leaves. It thrives in all but the poorest soils in full or part shade – golden-leaved varieties colour best in a little sunshine. Of the many varieties, two of the best for the small garden are *A. j.* 'Crotonifolia', which has green leaves brightly splashed with gold and is excellent for winter colour, and *A. j.* 'Rozannie', which bears dark green leaves and many large, bright red berries in autumn. Height and spread 1.2 m (4 feet).

An attractive evergreen that looks good even in the hardest winters is *Danäe racemosa* (Alexandrian laurel), which forms a low, spreading clump of arching shoots covered with narrow, shiny leaves. To keep it looking fresh it's best to trim off the old shoots in summer. Bright orange-red fruits may be produced after a hot summer. It's equally happy in sun or shade and prefers a good, retentive soil. Height and spread 60 cm (2 ft).

One of the most useful and tolerant evergreens for foliage colour is *Euonymus fortunei*, which makes good ground cover in either sun or shade on all but exceptionally poor or boggy soils. *E. f.* 'Emerald 'n' Gold' has deep green leaves brightly edged with gold, and *E. f.* 'Emerald Gaiety' boasts green leaves with a white margin – the leaves of both varieties are tinted pink in winter. *E. f.* 'Sunspot' produces green leaves with a long, central splash of gold. Height 45 cm (18 inches), spread 60 cm (2 feet).

Pachysandra terminalis makes good, evergreen ground cover for dry or moist shade, forming a carpet of fresh, glossy green leaves. It produces small spikes of greeny white flowers in late winter and early spring. Height 15 cm (6 inches), spread 45 cm (18 inches). There is a variegated form which can sulk at times and isn't nearly as attractive.

Ruscus aculeatus (butcher's broom) is tolerant of deep shade, forming dense clumps of thick, green stems topped with spiny, dark green 'leaves', which are really flattened stems. This evergreen shrub does well on dry soils of all types. Height and spread 60 cm (2 feet).

ACID-LOVING SHRUBS

If you're fortunate enough to have an acid soil, you'll be able to grow some wonderful plants including rhododendrons, azaleas, pieris and camellias. If your soil isn't naturally acid, don't attempt to make it so by using loads of peat – apart from the fact that it's a waste of a natural resource, your plants will eventually get their roots into your ordinary soil anyway and suffer a considerable shock! The best way to grow acid-lovers in limy conditions is to fill a raised bed with imported lime-free topsoil or grow plants in tubs of lime-free (ericaceous) potting compost.

Andromeda polifolia (bog rosemary) is an attractive, little, evergreen shrub with narrow, pointed leaves, bearing small, urn-shaped flowers in late spring and early summer. It does best in a moist soil. Both

A.p. 'Compacta' and *A.p.* 'Nikko' carry bright pink flowers and have neat, compact shapes. Height and spread 45 cm (18 inches).

Camellias brighten up a small garden in late winter and spring with their elegant, showy flowers, but these magnificent, glossy-leaved evergreens do need the right conditions to give of their best. In milder areas they prefer a lightly shaded site with an acid or neutral, moisture-retentive soil – Cornish gardens in particular are world-famous for their beautiful camellias. In colder areas they perform best in full sun and benefit from the protection of a sunny wall, but here in particular a good moisture-retentive soil is essential – a prime cause of bud drop before flowering is lack of water the previous summer and autumn when buds were just beginning to form. Camellias are actually a great deal tougher than is generally believed and can survive a surprising amount of frost. Severe frosts may disfigure flowers and foliage, so growing them in tubs for greenhouse and conservatory protection in winter is often the best practice in colder areas.

There are so many beautiful varieties now available that it's impossible to mention more than a few. Almost all are varieties of *Camellia japonica* or *C.* × *williamsii* and flower between late winter and late spring, tending towards spring flowering in colder areas. *C.* 'Donation' bears semi-double, clear pink flowers, while those of *C.* 'Anticipation' are deep rose-pink and 'paeony'-like. C. 'J. C. Williams' is a beautiful, paler pink, single-flowered variety. Many other varieties carry white, red or even bi-coloured flowers. C. japonica varieties – height 1.5 m (5 feet), spread 1.2 m (4 feet). C. × williamsii varieties – height 2.1 m (7 feet), spread 1.5 m (5 feet).

An exquisite and unusual camellia is C. sasanqua, which produces small, showy flowers from winter into early spring. It's not as hardy as those mentioned above; it requires a sheltered site in full sun and is best grown in a greenhouse or conservatory in all but the mildest areas. It's worth every bit of effort, however, to see its beautiful show of flowers in the dark days of winter. Two of the best varieties are C. 'Crimson King', with bright red, single flowers, and C. 'Narumi-gata', which bears large, fragrant, white flowers tinged with pink. Height 1.5 m (5 feet), spread 1.2 m (4 feet).

An exceptionally striking shrub for autumn colour is Fothergilla gardenii, which has rounded leaves that first turn yellow and orange, then become tinted with shades of scarlet and red until the whole bush appears to be on fire. Weather permitting, this colourful display lasts for several weeks until the leaves fall. In spring spiky clusters of sweetly scented flowers are borne on the branch tips. This shrub has a neat, rounded habit and can also be grown in a tub. It likes sun or part shade. Height 1 m (3 feet), spread 60 cm (2 feet).

Gaultheria procumbens (checkerberry) is a creeping shrub that forms a carpet of small, evergreen leaves. Little, urn-shaped flowers in late spring are followed by bright red berries in autumn. It prefers part or full shade in a fairly moist soil. Height 15 cm (6 inches), spread 1 m (3 feet).

Pieris are attractive evergreens for year-round interest, with flower buds developing in autumn and opening into urn-shaped flowers in mid- to late spring. These honey-scented flowers are popular with bees. Some pieris produce variegated foliage, and some have red or bronze, young shoots, which are particularly showy in spring but may be damaged by late frosts. Pieris need a good, moisture-retentive soil and light shade. Pieris japonica 'Purity' bears pure white flowers, which are shown off well against its fresh green foliage. Two of the best variegated pieris are P.j. 'Little Heath', with green and creamy white leaves, and P. 'Flaming Silver', which has bright red, young leaves that develop a handsome, white margin; both have creamy-white flowers. Height and spread 1 m (3 feet).

The genus Rhododendron is so vast that only a mere inkling of the varieties available can be given here. For the small garden, suitable rhododendrons are really only the dwarf varieties, R. yakushimanum hybrids and evergreen hybrid azaleas. All are evergreens with glossy leaves, suitable for tubs as well as borders, and the smallest varieties can also be used in rock gardens.

Far left: Rhododendron yakushimanum is one of the most attractive dwarf varieties, whose large silver-dusted leaves look good all year.

Left: R. 'Rosebud' with its bright pink flowers is just one of the many different Japanese azaleas available.

'Dwarf rhododendron' is a general term for those small-leaved hybrids and species with a height and spread of around 60 cm (2 feet). The following hybrids, which flower in mid- to late spring, give an idea of the colour range available: R. 'Baden Baden' has deep red flowers; R. 'Blue Diamond' and R. 'Blue Tit' bear lavender-blue ones; R. 'Bow Bells' is shell-pink; R. 'Cowslip' is creamy yellow; R. 'Pink Drift' is mauve-pink; and R. 'Scarlet Wonder' is ruby-red.

R. *yakushimanum* is a superb species with large, compact trusses of bell-shaped flowers in late spring. These are dark rose-pink in bud, opening to a beautiful shade of apple-blossom pink, which finally fades almost to white. The young growths are silvery; the dark green leaves are comparatively large and with a brown, 'woolly' layer underneath. This species is the parent of many superb hybrids boasting attractive and often unusual flower colours. They're especially good as their large leaves look more like those of a larger rhododendron than the small-leaved dwarfs, yet are compact with a height and spread of around 1 m (3 feet). Varieties include: R. 'Dusty Miller', with its pale pink flowers flushed red and fading to cream; R. 'Grumpy', which is cream lightly tinged with pink and spotted with orange-yellow inside; R. 'Surrey Heath', with pale rose-pink flowers deepening at the edges; and R. 'Titian Beauty', bearing waxy-red flowers. There are many other excellent hybrids.

Also part of the *Rhododendron* genus are evergreen hybrid azaleas, or Japanese azaleas, which comprise an enormous range of different hybrids that are a glorious sight in mid- to late spring, when laden with brightly coloured flowers. These rounded small-leaved shrubs do best in partial shade, sheltered from strong winds. There are many different colours including R. 'Blue Danube' carries bluish-violet flowers and R. 'Mother's Day' bright red. R. 'Blaauw's Pink' is bright salmon-pink and R. 'Niagara' bears white flowers. Height and spread 1 m (3 feet).

5

ROSES

The rose is one of our most familiar and best-loved flowers with a history that goes back for many hundreds of years. It has inspired poets, playwrights and lovers as well as gardeners, and the full-blown beauty of the flowers with their sweet, drifting fragrance is, to many people, the very essence of an English, summer garden.

In a small garden roses should be used carefully if colour and interest all year are your main aims – the outstanding beauty of their flowers is really their only attribute, and in winter their prickly, naked stems can look rather stark. To overcome this dilemma, it is necessary to abandon the traditional idea of a rose bed; instead incorporate roses in a mixed border, where other plants can camouflage their winter nudity. The formal flower shapes of large-flowered and cluster-flowered, modern bush roses (formerly known as hybrid teas and floribundas) aren't really suitable for the relaxed style of a mixed border, so choose varieties such as the English roses with more informal flowers, which go well with other plants.

Growing roses in a mixed border has other advantages. Pests and diseases are diluted and plants such as fennel can be used to attract natural predators of aphids, whereas disease can be combatted by selecting varieties that are naturally resistant and by ensuring plants have good growing conditions, as strong, healthy plants are much less susceptible to disease.

Roses do best in full sun on a fertile, well-drained soil; the only conditions they positively dislike are very wet clay, severely chalky soil or very damp, acid, peaty soil. They love an annual mulch of compost or well-rotted manure which contains some nutrients, and applications of high potash fertilizer which boosts flowering. If you're digging up old roses, never plant new roses in their place as specific pests and diseases will have built up in the soil over the years.

Rosa 'Surrey' is one of a new breed of long-flowering ground-cover roses. Roses associate extremely well with a number of herbaceous perennials, including the silver, woolly leaves of Stachys lanata which is planted behind this rose.

Of the many hundreds of roses of different types, sizes and colours, a good proportion are too large for a small garden or have only a short period of flower. I've chosen a few of the best performers from each group; early to mid-summer are their real months of glory, though the majority mentioned here give repeat flushes of flower throughout summer. For easy reference I have grouped the roses in this chapter according to their habit into: climbing and rambling roses; bush roses; and ground-cover roses. All sizes given below are those reached in approximately 10 years.

Most garden centres have space for only a limited number of the more popular varieties, but good specialist rose growers will supply plants by mail order in autumn or winter. The best time to buy is late autumn when the new season's stocks have become available.

CLIMBING AND RAMBLER ROSES

There's a place in virtually every garden for climbing roses, which divide into two distinct sub-groups – climbers and ramblers – that have different growing habits and methods of pruning. Both can be paired with other climbers that flower earlier or later to extend their season of interest, or they can both flower at the same time to make an exuberant display of colour. Large-flowered clematis are good partners for roses – try the massed, blue flowers of *Clematis* 'Perle d'Azur' with the pale pink rose *Rosa* 'New Dawn', for example. Annual climbers are good too: sweet peas with roses make a fragrant, cottage-garden display.

CLIMBING ROSES

Climbing roses have comparatively large flowers borne either singly or in small clusters. They're best grown on walls or fences as they build up a framework of rigid, main branches producing the lateral shoots that bear flowers. (The main branches should be trained fanwise or almost horizontally to stimulate the growth of laterals.) If your windowsills are more than 1 m (3 feet) above the ground, try planting a rose directly under the window and training it up either side.

Modern climbing rose varieties have mostly been introduced over the last 30 years. Most have repeat flushes of flower throughout summer. One of the best is *R.* 'Golden Showers' with its semi-double blooms of bright golden-yellow; it also does well in shade or sun. *R.* 'Handel' carries unusual, bi-coloured, small, semi-double flowers, creamy white edged with pink. *R.* 'Maigold' is a superb rose, displaying masses of bronze-yellow, semi-double flowers, which are strongly scented; this is a tough variety that does well in poor conditions. *R.* 'Parkdirektor Riggers' bears large clusters of mostly single, crimson flowers against glossy green foliage and is a very good repeat floworer. R. 'Pink Perpétue' produces clusters of double, rich pink flowers with a delicate fragrance. Height 3 m (10 feet).

Climbing miniature roses bear many clusters of small flowers in repeat flushes through summer. R. 'Laura Ford' has small, yellow flowers, which deepen to amberyellow later in the summer; R. 'Warm Welcome' is bright orange-red; and R. 'Rosalie Coral' carries orange-and-yellow flowers. Height 1.8 m (6 feet).

Classic, old-fashioned roses have gorgeous, usually fragrant flowers that are a crammed mass of petals. Some are excellent repeat flowerers. Good varieties include R. 'Gloire de Dijon' (old glory rose), a richly scented favourite with buff-yellow flowers tinted with pink and gold, and R. 'Madame Alfred Carrière', which bears masses of sweetly scented, cupped flowers, white flushed with pink. R. 'Zéphirine Drouhin' produces profuse quantities of fragrant, deep rose-pink flowers and does well on sunny or shady walls; it also has the rare asset of being almost completely thornless. It is, however, susceptible to disease. Height 4.5–6 m (15–20 feet).

Pergolas are ideal for rambling roses and other climbers. Later in the summer this pergola will be completely smothered by a rambling rose, making this a fragrant and sheltered seating area.

RAMBLER ROSES

Rambler roses produce masses of tiny flowers in large clusters, usually over a shorter period than climbing roses. They send up long, flexible shoots from the base of the plant, and some dense, older growth should be removed after flowering. Ramblers are more suited to arches, pergolas and pillars than climbing roses, and can also be grown through a mature tree or hedge. Several popular varieties such as R. 'Dorothy Perkins', however, are very susceptible to mildew. Good varieties include R. 'Albertine', which has trusses of large, semi-double, coppery pink flowers with a strong fragrance, and R. 'Crimson Shower', with its clusters of small, bright crimson flowers that show off well against its dark, shiny foliage. R. 'Goldfinch' is a lovely, fragrant variety bearing many clusters of small, warm yellow flowers becoming creamy white with age. R. 'New Dawn' is one of the loveliest, with clusters of large, silvery-pink blooms that have a fresh apple scent, as do those of R. 'Sander's White', which are small, semi-double and pure white. R. 'Seagull' bears masses of single, pure white blooms with golden stamens and is deliciously scented. Height 3–4.5 m (10–15 feet).

BUSH ROSES

Smallest of all bush roses are miniatures, which grow 30–45 cm (12–18 inches) high and have tiny clusters of flowers. Although they're good for tubs, they do tend to lack substance and it's often better to go for something a little larger. Dwarf, cluster-flowered bush roses – generally described as patio roses – are often the best option. These form compact, little bushes bearing many trusses of small flowers, and are ideal for tubs and small borders. R. 'Anna Ford' carries semi-double, orange-red flowers with golden stamens. R. 'Gentle Touch' produces pale pink flowers while those of R. 'Little Bo-Peep' are dainty pale pink. R. 'Perestroika' has double, golden-yellow blooms. R. 'Queen Mother' bears soft pink, semi-double flowers and R. 'Robin Redbreast' has dark crimson, yellow-centred ones. R. 'Sweet Dream' is an excellent rose with neatly cupped peachy apricot blooms. R. 'Top Marks' has brilliant orange-red flowers. Height and spread 45–60 cm (18–24 inches).

ENGLISH ROSES

Lovers of old-fashioned roses will welcome this newer group bred by rose specialist David Austin, who has combined the simple, old-fashioned charm and delicious fragrance of the old shrub roses with the repeat-flowering qualities and wider colour range of modern bush roses. There are now more than 70 varieties of English rose. R. 'Evelyn', one of the newest varieties with cup-shaped, richly fragrant flowers, displays flowers of a lovely blend of apricot and yellow. R. 'Perdita' has apricot-blush flowers.

R. 'St Cecilia' is pale apricot-pink. R. 'Sharifa Asma' is palest blush pink fading almost to white. R. 'Kathryn Morley' has soft pink flowers.

Those English roses with richly coloured flowers include: R. 'Pretty Jessica', which is deep pink; R. 'The Countryman', clear rose-pink; R. 'L. D. Braithwaite', brilliant crimson; and R. 'The Prince', which is rich crimson maturing to deep royal purple. There are some excellent yellows: R. 'Jayne Austin', with its attractive, soft yellow flowers with a hint of apricot; R. 'Yellow Button', which has soft yellow flowers splashed with darker yellow in the centre. Height and spread 1 m (3 ft).

OLD-FASHIONED SHRUB ROSES

The old-fashioned shrub roses have beautifully shaped, scented flowers; their disadvantage is that most either grow too large or flower for only a short time. There are several groups of old-fashioned roses, however, which are compact and produce repeat flushes of flowers. Dwarf polyantha roses are charming varieties with many bunches of small flowers. One of the best is R. 'The Fairy', a graceful, little shrub covered with tiny, pale pink flowers from mid-summer to autumn. The Portland roses are all compact bushes that repeat flower well. R. 'Little White Pet' bears clusters of pompon-type, white blooms densely packed with petals and is delicately scented. Height and spread 0.6–1 m (2–3 feet).

GROUND-COVER ROSES

Recently a number of ground-cover roses have been introduced in response to the demand for low-maintenance plants, both for large-scale landscaping and the ordinary garden. Ground-cover roses need little pruning and make a superb flowering carpet to edge a border or clothe a bank; the smallest varieties can even be used in tubs. There are some very vigorous varieties, especially the gamebird varieties – R. 'Pheasant', R. 'Grouse' and R. 'Partridge', which should be avoided in a small garden.

The County series of ground-cover roses flower from early summer well into autumn. R. 'Essex' which boasts a neat, dense habit and rich pink flowers that show off well against glossy green foliage. R. 'Hampshire' has warm scarlet flowers, with golden stamens, followed by orange hips in autumn. R. 'Kent' bears its pure white flowers in large clusters, while the double, bright yellow blooms of R. 'Norfolk' are scented. R. 'Sussex' carries large trusses of double, pale apricot flowers. Other good ground-cover roses include: R. 'Nozomi', with its many small, pearly pink flowers; R. 'Suma', which is bright pink; and R. 'Snow Carpet', a dainty rose with tiny, double, pure white blooms from early summer to mid-autumn. Height 30–60 cm (1–2 feet), spread 0.6–1.2 m (2–4 feet).

6

CLIMBERS AND WALL SHRUBS

Ground space in a small garden may be limited, but virtually every garden has walls and fences perfect for clothing in all manner of colourful climbers and wall shrubs. All too often the only way to go is up, and vertical gardening has enormous potential for giving the garden extra colour and interest.

Climbers have a wealth of uses elsewhere in the garden too. Compost heaps and other garden paraphernalia can easily be concealed by trellis screens clothed with climbers. Plant-covered archways make a delightful garden entrance or a definitive boundary between different parts of the garden – fragrant climbers on arches emit wafts of scent as you pass through. And what could be more pleasant than to sit in the dappled shade of a plant-covered pergola or arbour on a hot, sunny day, breathing in the delicious fragrance of roses, honeysuckle or jasmine.

Established shrubs, trees and conifers can be threaded with climbing plants for an extra garlanding of summer colour, but, in these situations, avoid planting strong-growing climbers, which can quickly entwine their hosts in a fatal grip. It's best to use less vigorous ones such as annual varieties, large-flowered clematis or *Lathyrus latifolius*, the perennial pea.

Climbing plants can be divided into those such as ivy that are self-clinging, and those with twining stems, tendrils or long, scrambling stems, which need some form of support in order to climb. Check your walls before planting self-clinging climbers; on older walls where mortar may be soft the aerial roots can work their way into any cracks and hasten deterioration but, where mortar is sound, there should be no problems.

Evergreen climbers and wall shrubs make perfect nesting sites for birds – the term wall shrub being generally used to describe shrubs such as pyracanthas that can be trained to grow up a wall or fence. In garden

Climbing plants completely cover the walls of this town garden, creating a lush environment. The bulk of the right-hand wall is covered by the vigorous climber *Humulus lupulus* 'Aureus' (golden hop).

centres wall shrubs are usually displayed alongside the climbing plants.

When siting wall shrubs, bear in mind that some do grow bulky with age. Plant vigour must also be considered in relation to each site for a wall shrub or climber: if you only have a strip of wall 1 m (3 feet) wide to cover, then a fast-growing *Clematis montana* is not for you. One plant to avoid at all costs is the incredibly rampant *Polygonum baldschuanicum* (Russian vine), which certainly isn't called mile-a-minute for nothing! Beware of using vigorous climbers on fences too, as in time the sheer weight of the plant could prove too great. A number of vigorous plants have been included here, so make sure you choose the right ones for each situation. All sizes given below are those attained after approximately 10 years.

Support for plants can be provided in many ways. Trellis is available in different shapes and materials, the choice of which depends on your taste and budget. When fixing trellis, use wooden battens to form a 25 mm (1 inch) gap between the trellis and the wall or fence, so that the plants have room to twine. A cheaper option to trellis is plastic mesh, but this can quickly become worn and unattractive. On walls the cheapest and most effective support is strong wire run through vine eyes (metal pins with eyelets) – if run along the mortar courses of a wall, the wire can barely be seen.

Before planting, plenty of organic matter needs to be incorporated in the soil; at the base of walls in particular the soil receives little rain and can be very dry. Placing the plant at least 30 cm (1 foot) away from the wall helps it get more water.

Aspect is the critical factor when choosing climbers and wall shrubs. It can be very clearly defined according to which way the planting site faces. Here plants are divided into those for north- or east-facing sites, south- or west-facing sites and sheltered, south-facing walls.

NORTH- OR EAST-FACING SITES

Such sites are generally shaded and so have a reputation for being unduly difficult to plant. In fact there are plenty of plants for both flower and foliage colour that happily flourish away from the sun. With only a couple of exceptions, all these plants also do equally well in south- or west-facing sites.

One of the first to flower in spring is *Chaenomeles* (Japanese quince, cydonia or japonica) which is an excellent, easily grown, deciduous shrub that can be easily trained to brighten up a shady wall. It grows readily on all but chalky soil. Saucer-shaped flowers are borne in clusters all along the naked stems throughout spring, followed in autumn by edible fruits, which can be used in preserves. Prune outward-pointing

Nearest the house *Hedera colchica* 'Dentata Variegata' (Persian ivy) mingles with the purple flowers of *Clematis viticella* 'Etoile Violette'. *Jasminum officinale* 'Aureum' is growing on the right-hand wall.

shoots back to 2–3 buds immediately after flowering and again in late summer. A lovely variety is C. × superba 'Crimson and Gold', with its deep red petals and a golden centre. C. × s. 'Knap Hill Scarlet' carries bright orange-red flowers and those of C. × s. 'Pink Lady' – an early flowerer – are rose-pink. C. speciosa 'Nivalis' has large, pure white flowers. Chaenomeles make a lovely spring display when planted with early-flowering herbaceous perennials such as pulmonaria, Helleborus orientalis and bergenias. Height 1.8 m (6 feet).

Large-flowered clematis with bi-coloured flowers do best away from the sun, which can bleach their delicately coloured blooms. Best known is Clematis 'Nelly Moser', which carries large, pale lilac-pink flowers with a central bar of deep pink on each petal. There are, however, lots of other lesser-known varieties that are equally handsome: C. 'Capitaine Thuilleaux' has flowers striped deep pink with a pale creamy pink background; C. 'Barbara Jackman' bears pale blue-mauve petals with a deep red bar; and the flowers of C. 'Carnaby' are deep raspberry-pink with a darker pink bar. Height 1.8–2.4 m (6–8 feet). Many other clematis, especially paler varieties, flower well in an easterly situation but dislike very shady, north-facing sites. Some of these are described in the next section (south- or west-facing sites).

Cotoneaster horizontalis (herring-bone cotoneaster) is a tough, deciduous shrub widely used for ground cover but is equally happy hugging a wall, given a little encouragement to grow in the right direction. As its name suggests, the stems form a 'fishbone' pattern that looks attractive all year round. Small, white flowers in spring are followed by masses of red berries strung along the branches like beads; at the same time the tiny leaves turn bright glowing red to make a really fiery display. Height 2.4 m (8 feet).

Toughest of all evergreen foliage climbers are Hedera (ivies) with glossy, attractive foliage. There are many varieties which display an enormous range of leaf shapes and colours. Ivies thrive in all conditions from full sun to deep shade, even under difficult circumstances such as poor, dry soil. Ivies are self-clinging, and also make excellent ground-cover plants if grown without support. Hedera colchica (Persian ivy) is a handsome and vigorous, large-leaved species. One of its most attractive varieties is H.c. 'Sulphur Heart' (also known as 'Paddy's Pride') with large, dark green leaves interestingly coloured with a bold, central splash of pale lime-green. H.c. 'Dentata Variegata' has bright green leaves strikingly edged creamy white; the mature leaves are often elongated, giving an established plant the appearance of gracefully draping itself over its support. Height and spread 5.1 m (17 feet).

H. helix is a small-leaved species that comes in an enormous range of varieties. H.h. 'Goldheart' is deservedly popular with its neat, dark green leaves splashed in the centre with bright yellow – it is excellent for brightening a gloomy corner. A plant for the patient gardener is slow-growing *H.h.* 'Buttercup', which boasts pure golden leaves that colour best in sun. Some varieties such as *H.h.* 'Cavendishii' have green leaves mottled with white, while those of *H.h.* 'Glacier' are edged with white. Others produce attractively shaped leaves of plain green; the leaf edges of *H.h.* 'Green Ripple', for example, are jagged and each leaf has a long, tapering central lobe. Heights vary accord-

The golden flowers of *Jasminum nudiflorum* are lovely for winter colour, especially combined with the fragile beauty of snowdrops.

ing to the variety: as a general guide the more green on the leaf, the faster the rate of growth. Height (of fastest varieties) 3.6 m (12 feet).

For a real splash of winter cheer there is little to beat *Jasminum nudiflorum* (winter jasmine), a delightful, easily grown shrub bearing numerous stars of bright yellow flowers on its naked branches from early winter through to early spring. Unlike the summer-flowering varieties the flowers have no scent. Long growths should be cut hard back immediately after flowering to maintain a good shape and encourage plenty of flowering shoots for next season. Winter jasmine also does well on pillars, providing its shoots are tied in regularly. Height and spread 1.8 m (6 feet).

Lonicera × *tellmanniana* (honeysuckle) is a gorgeous, showy, deciduous variety, which does best in part or full shade. The rich deep yellow flowers, flushed red in bud, are up to 5 cm (2 inches) long and borne in profuse clusters in early to mid-summer. The only disappointment is its lack of scent, but the delight to the eye more than makes up for any shortfall to the nose. Height 3.6 m (12 feet).

One of the best climbers for fiery autumn colour is *Parthenocissus henryana*, a vigorous creeper that is the most ornamental of the *Parthenocissus* varieties. The leaves are separated into three to five, dark green leaflets on which the veins are traced in silver, giving a lovely marbled effect. In autumn the foliage turns glowing shades of red, holding for several weeks before carpeting the ground. Its stems develop self-clinging adhesive pads, though it may well need some initial training. Height 4.8 m (16 feet).

Pyracantha (firethorn) is a vigorous, thorny, evergreen shrub that bears masses of white, hawthorn-like flower clusters in late spring and early summer. In autumn it is festooned with clusters of glowing, red, orange or yellow berries, which show up beautifully against its small, glossy leaves. Birds love the red and orange berries in particular. Good varieties include: *P.* 'Orange Glow', with its orange-red berries; *P.* 'Orange Charmer' has deep orange berries, while those of *P.* 'Soleil d'Or' (also known as 'Golden Sun') are yellow. *P.* 'Red Column' carries scarlet berries and *P.* 'Shawnee' has yellow and pale orange ones, which colour early. Height 3.6 m (12 feet). There are also variegated varieties such as *P.* 'Harlequin' and *P.* 'Sparkler' – these dislike shade and need a sunny, sheltered position. Height 1.8 m (6 feet).

A connoisseur's plant – tricky to grow but guaranteed to attract attention – is *Tropaeolum speciosum* (Scotch flame flower). In summer and autumn it is covered in masses of small, rich bright scarlet flowers. The slender, scrambling stems, which are clothed in small, fresh green, lobed leaves, die back to ground level in winter. Scotch flame flower is perfect for growing through dark-foliaged plants, particularly conifers, and can be seen in its full glory at

The white spring flowers of *Pyracantha coccinea* (firethorn) are followed in autumn by masses of glowing red berries.

Hidcote Gardens in Gloucestershire growing through a yew hedge. It grows best in cooler parts of Britain; elsewhere it and should be set against a north-facing wall or hedge, in an acid soil, which should always be cool and moist. Height 3 m (10 feet).

SOUTH- OR WEST-FACING SITES

These situations are sunnier than north- or east-facing sites and are suitable for growing a great range of plants for both flower and foliage colour. Most of the climbers and wall shrubs in the previous section will be happy here, as will climbing and rambler roses and annual climbers.

For unusual foliage colour *Actinidia kolomikta* is a real stunner, with slender stems covered in heart-shaped leaves tri-coloured in green, cream and pink, looking like a dramatic painter's palette. The faint smell given off by the plant is often irresist-ible to cats, who may have something to do with this plant's slow rate of establishment, and some protection with net or wire is advisable in its early years. It prefers a moist, well-drained soil. Height 3–3.9 m (10–13 feet).

Nothing can beat clematis for sheer versa-tility and variety, and it would be hard to have too many of these colourful garden glories. These deciduous climbers can be planted in all sorts of places: walls, fences, arches, tripods, growing through shrubs and trees, as well as with other climbers such as roses. Two large-flowered hybrids can even be grown together in the same spot to give a really long season of flower. Having their roots in the shade and their heads in the sun is the perfect position for clematis, especi-ally the large-flowered varieties. In a sunny site, shade the roots with stones or ground-cover plants. Clematis prefer well-drained soil enriched with organic matter; the large-flowered hybrids in particular are hungry plants that benefit from plenty of feeding and a little added lime on neutral or acid soils. Less vigorous varieties can be grown in tubs so long as their roots are shaded.

When all or part of a clematis plant sud-denly collapses and dies back, it may be suf-fering from 'clematis wilt' – a disease that occasionally affects large-flowered hybrids. There is no reliable prevention or cure. The best precaution is to plant the top of the clematis rootball 8 cm (3 inches) below soil level so, if affected, the clematis will usually send up new shoots from below the ground.

Large-flowered hybrid clematis carry showy flowers, 10–20 cm (4–8 inches) across, in a wide range of colours: white, blue, pink, red or purple. By selecting a suc-cession of varieties you can have flowers from early summer until autumn. Choice of varieties is very much down to individual colour preferences. I particularly like blue varieties. *Clematis* 'Perle d'Azur' produces magnificent masses of azure-blue flowers from summer to autumn; C. 'Elsa Späth' bears large, lavender-purple flowers in early summer and again in autumn, as does C. 'H. F. Young', which is a lovely Wedgwood-blue with creamy white stamens. C. 'The President' carries deep purple-blue flowers from late spring to early autumn and has been deservedly popular for more than 100 years. C. 'Vyvyan Pennell' is a superb, double-flowered variety with rosette-like flowers of deep lavender-blue in mid-sum-mer and again in autumn. Height 1.8–2.4 m (6–8 feet).

White clematis are excellent for growing through dark-foliaged plants, where their flowers appear almost luminous in the dusk. 'Marie Boisselot' (also known as 'Madame le Coultre') is an excellent variety bearing

masses of pure white flowers from early summer to early autumn. C. 'Miss Bateman' has white flowers with prominent reddish stamens in late spring and early summer. C. 'Henryi' is an old variety producing white

Lonicera 'Baggesen's Gold' with its golden foliage makes a perfect host for a dark blue *Clematis* X *durandii*. In the foreground two small shrubs – *Euonymus* 'Emerald 'n' Gold' and a purple-leaved berberis – make a good combination.

flowers with contrasting brown anthers in early summer and, again, in early autumn. Reds and pinks look especially good associated with golden-foliaged shrubs; C. 'Niobe' has velvety, deep ruby-red flowers with contrasting creamy stamens from early summer to early autumn; despite the deep colour it fades very little in full sunshine. C. 'Comtesse de Bouchaud' is one of the best pinks, bearing profuse quantities of deep silvery pink flowers in mid- to late summer. C. 'Pink Champagne' carries silvery pink flowers in late spring followed by deeper pink flowers in late summer. Height 1.8-2.4 m (6-8 feet).

For sheer charm and delicacy there is little to beat the small-flowered species clematis. Their many shaped and coloured flowers are generally up to 8 cm (3 inches) across, but they are mostly more vigorous than the large-flowered hybrids – some much more so, as in the case of C. montana. C. alpina is lovely for early spring colour with delicate, nodding, blue flowers borne on slender stalks in mid- to late spring, followed by fluffy seed heads. This tough, easily pleased species thrives in sun or shade. C.a. 'Frances Rivis' produces large, blue flowers, up to 5 cm (2 inches) long with contrasting, white stamens. C.a. 'Ruby' bears rosy-red flowers. Height 1.8-3 m (6-10 feet).

C. montana is an exceptionally vigorous species, which should be sited with care; if you have an old shed to cover, for example, this plant will do the job admirably! It's happy in all aspects including north-facing sites, and is a glorious sight in late spring smothered in a profusion of white flowers. In late spring and early summer C.m. var. rubens displays rose-pink flowers, which are attractively enhanced against its bronze-purple foliage. C.m. 'Elizabeth' has soft pink flowers with a delicate vanilla scent. Height 6-9 m (20-30 feet).

Two excellent, late-flowering species are C. tangutica and C. viticella. From mid-summer to mid-autumn the deep yellow, lantern-shaped flowers of C. tangutica are shown off beautifully against its divided, sea-green foliage. Flowers are followed by showy, silken seed heads, which make an extra backcloth to the later flowers. C. viticella also bears masses of nodding flowers, from late summer onwards, and is a good variety to grow with roses as they can both be hard pruned at the same time in early spring. Good varieties include: C.v. 'Alba Luxurians', with its white, mauve-tinged flowers; C.v. 'Abundance' has delicate, purple flowers; and C.v. 'Purpurea Plena Elegans' carries double, lilac-purple flowers. Height 3-3.9 m (10-13 feet).

A golden backcloth is the ideal setting for many garden plants, and the large soft yellow leaves of Humulus lupulus 'Aureus' (golden hop) look lovely both in their own right and as a backing for other darker-foliaged plants. This fast-growing climber, with its long, twining stems, does best on a pergola, tripod or fence, and dies back to ground level each winter. Height 3–4.8 m (10–16 feet) each year, once established.

Fragrant climbers are among my favourites and the delicious scent of *Jasminum officinale* (common white jasmine) has deservedly made it one of our most popular garden plants. This easily cultivated, deciduous climber has been grown in Britain for more than 400 years. It does well in shade or sun. Small white flowers are borne in clusters from early summer through to autumn. Plant this jasmine near a seating area or on a house wall where its lovely, coconut scent can drift in through an open window during the day and more strongly in the evening. *J.o.f.* 'Affine' has slightly larger flowers tinged with pink. Height 3.9 m (13 feet).

Lathyrus latifolius (perennial pea) is an immensely useful climber best grown through other plants rather than on its own. Magenta-pink 'sweet pea' blossoms borne in summer and early autumn look delightful peeping through the foliage of shrubs or conifers, and look especially good with grey and silver foliage. *L.l.* 'White Pearl' is a more unusual, pure white form. Unlike the annual sweet pea, the perennial pea has little or no fragrance. It dies back to ground level each autumn and, although tolerant of a wide range of soils, it's happiest on a well-drained soil. Height 1.8 m (6 feet) each year, once established.

Honeysuckle is a familiar, fragrant delight with its clusters of sweetly scented flowers in summer. It prefers a little shade, and its ideal position is to have shaded roots but with sun on its top. Most honeysuckles prefer a moist, well-drained soil. *Lonicera periclymenum* 'Belgica' (early Dutch honeysuckle) flowers in late spring and early summer, bearing clusters of reddish-purple and white flowers fading to yellow. This variety – like *L.p.* 'Serotina' and *L.j.* 'Halliana', below – does well in dry soils given plenty of organic matter. *L.p.* 'Harlequin' has leaves variegated in cream, pink and green. *L.p.* 'Serotina' (late Dutch honeysuckle) carries deep reddish-purple and white flowers from mid-summer to mid-autumn. From early summer to early autumn, *L.p.* 'Graham Thomas' bears profuse quantities of flowers, which are white at first then changing to yellow. *L.* × *heckrottii* (also known as *L.* 'Gold Flame') is a showy variety producing large clusters of deep glowing yellow flowers, flushed with yellow-orange, also from early summer to early autumn. Height 3.9 m (13 feet).

All the above varieties are deciduous, but *L. japonica* 'Halliana' (Japanese honeysuckle) retains its leaves in all but the hardest winters. Small clusters of deliciously scented, white-and-yellow flowers are profusely borne from early summer to autumn. This plant is superb for covering unsightly objects, especially the stark lines of chain-link fencing. Height 4.8 m (16 feet).

Wisteria is a real garden aristocrat and a

breathtaking sight festooned with long racemes of fragrant flowers in late spring and early summer. *Wisteria floribunda* (Japanese wisteria) is perfect for walls, pergolas or for growing into an old tree. Its large, pinnate, deciduous leaves add an oriental touch. Although there are varieties with white or pink flowers, nothing can really improve on those with beautiful, blue flowers such as the dark blue *W.f.* 'Domino' or the violet-blue *W.f.* 'Violacea Plena'. For a really dramatic display, *W.f. macrobotrys* (also known as 'Multijuga') bears enormous racemes of pale blue flowers up to 1 m (3 feet) long. If growing this variety on an arch or pergola, make the structure higher than usual to allow for the drop of the flowers. Height 3.9 m (13 feet). Unless you have lots of wall space, avoid *W. sinensis* (Chinese wisteria) because it is very vigorous. An interesting way to identify the above wisteria species is to see which direction the stems twine: *W. floribunda* twines clockwise while *W. sinensis* twines anti-clockwise! When purchasing wisteria, check that plants have been produced by grafting – those raised from seed may take many years to flower.

SHELTERED, SOUTH-FACING WALLS

If you have a warm, south-facing wall sheltered from strong winds or if you live in a milder area you can grow some exceptionally lovely climbers and wall shrubs. However, if you want a garden that more or less takes care of itself then these plants are not for you, as in hard winters they may need a little cosseting, especially in colder areas. Tucking straw or dry bracken around the base of a plant in winter may mean the difference between its survival and death. In very severe winters there is always the risk of losing a plant completely, but more often than not they come through and give an unrivalled and exuberant display of colour. To allow plenty of time for these climbers and wall shrubs to establish before winter, planting is best done in spring. Most of these plants should be stocked by good garden centres but they may have to be purchased from specialist nurseries.

Campsis (trumpet vine) is a vigorous, exotic, deciduous climber with gorgeous, trumpet-shaped flowers, up to 8 cm (3 inches) long, borne in huge, drooping panicles on the ends of the stems in late summer and early autumn. The large, fresh green leaves make an attractive foil to the flowers. It's best to avoid placing other plants in front of this climber, as the whole of the trumpet vine needs maximum sunshine. *C. radicans* 'Yellow Trumpet' has rich yellow flowers and mostly climbs by means of aerial roots, though it needs support at first. *C.* × *tagliabuana* 'Madame Galen' produces bright orange-red flowers and needs support throughout its life. Height 4.5 m (15 feet).

Two magnificent, evergreen clematis need a sheltered site to give of their best.

Clematis armandii is a handsome and vigorous plant with large, glossy, leathery leaves and many clusters of small, delicately scented, white flowers in mid- to late spring. *C.a.* 'Apple Blossom' boasts white flowers washed with pink inside and mauve-pink outside. Height 3.9–4.8 m (13–16 feet). *C. cirrhosa* var. *balearica* (fern-leaved clematis) is a winter-flowering gem, bearing nodding, pale yellow flowers delicately spotted inside with red. The flowers are emphasized by its divided leaves, tinted bronze in winter. The flowers of *C.c.* 'Freckles' are splashed with red. Height 3–3.9 m (10–13 feet).

Eccremocarpus scaber (Chilean glory vine) dies back to ground level in winter in all except the mildest areas, and slender, scrambling stems grow rapidly from the base in spring. Through summer and autumn it makes a bright splash of colour, covered

Above: Clematis cirrhosa var. balearica is a winter-flowering beauty for a sunny, sheltered wall. The ferny leaves become tinted with bronze in winter.

Right: Fremontodendron 'California Glory' with its waxy golden flowers in summer is a magnificent plant which also needs a sunny wall.

with masses of small, tubular, orange-red or yellow flowers. Chilean glory vine can also be raised easily from seed and treated as an annual climber. Plants sown in early spring generally flower the same year. Height 1.8 m (6 feet) each year, once established.

One of the showiest of all wall shrubs is *Fremontodendron* 'California Glory' – a glorious sight in summer covered with golden, saucer-shaped, waxy flowers up to 7 cm (3 inches) across. The large, lobed, grey-green leaves are evergreen and covered in tiny hairs; beware these and the hairy seed capsules, which if handled may irritate the skin. A well-drained soil is essential, and it thrives on chalky soils. Fremontodendron needs generous space to spread, and can be trained closely against a wall. Height and spread 3.6–4.5 m (12–15 feet).

Some exotic varieties of jasmine, such as the two described here, need a sheltered site, or can be grown in a conservatory. Throughout spring, *Jasminum mesnyi* (primrose jasmine) bears semi-double, bright yellow flowers, up to 5 cm (2 inches) long, which show up well against its evergreen foliage. Height 3.6 m (12 feet). *J. officinale* 'Aureum' is a variety of the common white jasmine, with deciduous foliage strikingly variegated and flushed with yellow, making a bright, sunny display from spring to autumn. Scented, white flowers are carried in summer but much less profusely than for the common white jasmine. Height 2.4 m (8 feet).

The unusual, blue-and-white flowers of *Passiflora caerulea* (passion flower) make a real talking point. This fast-growing native of South America reputedly got its name because of the connection made by Spanish priests between the flowers and the instruments of the Crucifixion. The three stigmas are said to represent the three nails, the five anthers the five wounds, and so on. After a hot summer orange, egg-shaped fruits may be produced; the seeds and pulp are edible. In mild areas passion flowers retain most of their large, lobed leaves, but in hard winters may die back to the ground. They need a well-drained soil. *P.c.* 'Constance Elliott' is an outstanding variety with pure ivory-white flowers. Height 3–4.5 (10–15 feet).

Solanum jasminoides 'Album' is a beautiful, semi-evergreen climber. Clusters of elegant, cool white, 'potato' flowers, each with a central sheaf of yellow stamens, are borne amidst glossy green foliage from early summer until the first frosts. This vigorous, twining plant is ideal for a sheltered pergola as well as a wall. Height 4.8 m (16 feet).

Trachelospermum asiaticum is an evergreen, self-clinging climber bearing jasmine-like flowers in mid- to late summer. The flowers, which emit a delectable fragrance, open creamy white with a yellow centre, gradually changing completely to yellow as they mature. Trachelospermum grows neatly against a wall and prefers a slightly acid soil. Height 3 m (10 feet). *T. jasminoides* is more vigorous and less hardy.

7

CONIFERS

Conifers are perfect, low-maintenance plants for year-round interest, which really step into the limelight during the winter months. Conifers can be used in rockeries, tubs, for ground cover, screening, in a mixed border as a foil for other plants, or as accent plants.

The number of conifers you include in your garden depends very much on personal preference. A few years ago, low-maintenance borders or even whole gardens of conifers and heathers were very popular; though many people now prefer a greater variety of plants, conifers still have a valuable part to play in the garden, especially for winter colour: patio tubs of dwarf conifers, for example, planted with heathers, trailing ivies, winter-flowering pansies and perhaps *Skimmia japonica* 'Rubella' with its showy flower buds, make a supremely colourful display.

Larger conifers can be strategically placed for screening or as feature plants, either singly or in small groups. Conifers are frequently planted for hedges; one of my pet hates – the ubiquitous leyland cypress (×

Cupressocyparis leylandii) – has for many years been used as a horticultural cure-all wherever there's any need for screening. In small gardens the result is often nothing short of disastrous, as leyland cypresses relentlessly grow upwards at great speed and also attain considerable width. Generally I wouldn't recommend any tall conifer hedge for a small garden as such a solid block of foliage can be very dominating. However, if a high hedge is essential one of the best options is to plant a slower-growing, more ornamental variety such as × *C.* 'Gold Rider', with its bright gold foliage, or *Thuja plicata*, which responds well to trimming and will regrow if hard pruned into old wood.

As a general rule conifers grow well in most soils but dislike extreme conditions such as very shallow chalk, pure sand or

Conifers can be incorporated in a mixed border along with shrubs. Two tall *Chamaecyparis lawsoniana* varieties help build up an enduring framework either side of the border, and at the far end of the garden a golden conifer looks effective against the dark background.

boggy ground; they do best sited in full sun or light shade. Golden-foliaged varieties in particular dislike cold winds, and all newly planted conifers in exposed sites benefit from having a temporary windbreak of fine netting or polythene during their first year.

Conifers are described here in four groups; tall conifers; prostrate, spreading varieties; compact varieties; and dwarf conifers for tubs, troughs and small rockeries. All sizes given below are those reached in approximately 10 years. Do take care to check eventual size when buying – conifers look so innocent when small, but a plant that looks perfect for a windowbox may eventually threaten the view from an upstairs window!

TALL CONIFERS

Although the majority of tall conifers eventually attain a substantial spread as well as height, some do stay slender throughout their lives and these are the best varieties to have where space is limited. In winter the near-vertical branches of these slender conifers may become loaded with snow and get distorted or broken. Apart from going out in a blizzard and knocking accumulated snow off with a broom (which I've done on occasions to save precious plants!), an option less likely to result in frostbite is to wrap plants round loosely with large-mesh netting or green twine, which is soon covered by the growing plant.

Good, slender varieties of *Chamaecyparis*

lawsoniana (Lawson cypress) include 'Columnaris' (also known as 'Columnaris Glauca'), which forms a narrow, conical tree of dense, bluish foliage. *C.l.* 'Grayswood Feather' makes a slender column of dark green foliage, while *C.l.* 'Grayswood Gold' has the same shape but is golden yellow. Height 2.4m (8 feet), spread up to 1 m (3 feet).

Cupresus glabra 'Pyramidalis' (Arizona cypress), also called *C. arizonica* 'Conica', forms a narrow column of intense blue-grey foliage. The neat, slender, columnar shape of *C. sempervirens* (Italian or Mediterranean cypress), with its dark green foliage, is excellent for a formal garden. The foliage on *C.s.* 'Swane's Golden' is brightly tinged with gold. These varieties aren't suited to exposed situations. Height 2.1 m (7 feet), spread 60 cm–1 m (2–3 feet).

A hardier alternative is one of the narrowest of all conifers. *Juniperus scopulorum* 'Skyrocket', which develops a very slender column of blue-grey foliage, is excellent for providing an 'exclamation mark' in an area of low planting or to frame a path or view. Height 2.4 m (8 feet), spread 45 cm (18 inches).

PROSTRATE, SPREADING CONIFERS

Of the multitude of spreading conifers available, avoid the many vigorous varieties intent on wall-to-wall carpeting or those that eventually form a large, spreading mound. All conifers in this section are junipers, though the more vigorous varieties such as *Juniperus horizontalis* have not been included. There are some good, spreading varieties of *J. communis* (common juniper); *J.c.* 'Depressa Aurea' produces bright golden shoots in spring and early summer and makes excellent ground cover for a sunny site; *J.c.* 'Green Carpet' forms a dense ground-hugging mat of dark green foliage, which becomes bright green in summer. *J.c.* 'Hornibrookii', which has dark green leaves backed with silvery white, flows over the ground so closely that it shapes itself to any object it creeps over, lending an interesting texture to a border or rockery. Height 20 cm (8 inches), spread 1.2 m (4 feet).

J. conferta (shore juniper) is an excellent prostrate variety that creates a dense carpet of fresh apple-green foliage, which becomes bronze tinted in winter. *J.c.* 'Blue Pacific' produces blue-green foliage. Height 30 cm (1 foot), spread 1.2 m (4 feet). *J. procumbens* 'Nana' (creeping juniper) makes excellent ground cover and particularly likes a well-drained, sunny site. It forms a dense carpet of bluish-green foliage.

COMPACT CONIFERS

The wealth of handsome, compact conifers that grow to a maximum height of 1.2 m (4 feet) are ideal for borders, larger rockeries and tubs. Their enormous range of shapes and colours include some unusual varieties such as miniature pines and spruces.

Chamaecyparis lawsoniana (Lawson cypress) has many varieties with excellent, compact shapes. *C.l.* 'Aurea Densa' forms a conical bush of golden foliage, attractively arranged in rigid, flattened sprays. *C.l.* 'Ellwood's Pillar', with its feathery bluish foliage, height 1 m (3 feet), spread 45 cm (18 inches), is a narrower form of the popular *C.l.* 'Ellwoodii' while *C.l.* 'Pygmaea Argentea' is one of the best variegated varieties, with blue-green foliage tipped with silver. Height and spread 45 cm (18 inches). *C.l.* 'Minima Aurea' produces dense sprays of bright gold foliage and forms a neat cone shape. Height 60 cm (2 feet), spread 30 cm (1 foot). *C. obtusa* 'Nana Gracilis' (Hinoki cypress) is lovely for an oriental-style planting. Its dark green foliage is neatly arranged in scalloped sprays. Height and spread 60 cm (2 feet).

Juniperus squamata 'Blue Star' creates a compact, little bush of dense, silvery blue foliage. Height 20 cm (8 inches), spread 45 cm (18 inches).

Dwarf pines make attractive, little bushes of densely packed needles, which look far more like miniature trees than many other dwarf conifers. *Pinus mugo* varieties are all excellent dwarfs, forming low, wide-spreading mounds. My favourite is *P.m.* 'Ophir', which bears dark green needles touched with gold through summer and autumn. With the onset of winter it performs a real conjuring trick and turns bright gold all over. Height 45 cm (18 inches), spread 60 cm (2 feet). *P.m.* 'Winter Gold' is similar

but a little larger. Height 60 cm (2 feet), spread 1 m (3 feet).

A good, slow-growing, upright conifer is *Taxus baccata* 'Standishii' (golden yew) which makes a narrow column of golden foliage. Height 1 m (3 feet), spread 30 cm (1 foot).

Many *Thuja* varieties make marvellous border plants. Of the very distinctive golden varieties, *T. occidentalis* 'Rheingold' is the most popular. It forms a wide-spreading pyramid of gold foliage, turning a rich coppery gold in winter. Height 1.2 m (4 feet), spread 0.6–1 m (2–3 feet).

DWARF CONIFERS FOR TUBS, TROUGHS AND SMALL ROCKERIES

These dwarf conifers, growing to a maximum height of 60 cm (2 feet), are tailor-made feature plants for miniature landscapes. They come in all shapes and sizes – rounded 'bun' shapes, domes, low mounds, cylinders – and in many different foliage colours. Dwarf conifers with alpines and tiny bulbs make a wonderful display to grace any patio or rockery, and flower colours can be chosen as a contrast: deep blue gentians look wonderful with golden conifers, for example. Only junipers are happy in full sun all day; other conifers either need a little shade or can be placed in full sun so long as their roots are shaded with rock or stones.

Conifers look good in containers. Here a *Juniperus* 'Blue Star' and a golden heather in a terracotta pot add form to this corner of the border.

Because these varieties are extremely slow-growing, they tend to be fairly expensive.

There are some excellent, tiny forms of *Chamaecyparis pisifera* (Sawara cypress): 'Nana' forms a flat-topped, little mound of dense, dark blue-green, feathery foliage, while *C.p.* 'Nana Aureovariegata' is attractively tinged with gold and *C.p.* 'Nana Variegata' is splashed with creamy white. Height and spread 45 cm (18 inches).

Cryptomeria japonica 'Vilmoriniana' (dwarf Japanese cedar) creates a neat globe of dense, stiff, green foliage, turning a lovely shade of deep rust-red in winter. It should be placed away from cold winds. Height and spread 30 cm (1 foot).

One of the best of all the tiny dwarfs is *Juniperus communis* 'Compressa'. This forms a neat column of dense, grey-green foliage and really looks like a large tree in miniature. It loves a hot, sunny site and looks good with fleshy leaved alpines such as *Sempervivum*. Height 45 cm (18 inches), spread 15 cm (6 inches).

All the dwarf spruces look especially good in spring cloaked in their first flush of fresh green foliage. *Picea abies* 'Echiniformis' (dwarf spruce) produces a dense, low mound of needle-like, light green leaves, while the rounded dome of *P.a.* 'Gregoryana' comprises rich green foliage. *P.a.* 'Little Gem' is a neat bun shape. *P. glauca* 'Alberta Globe' makes a compact, rounded globe of light green foliage. Height and spread 30–45 cm (12–18 inches).

8

HERBACEOUS PERENNIALS

Herbaceous perennials are enjoying a resurgence in popularity as their potential for providing colour and form in the garden – and especially in the mixed border – begins to be fully realized. Perennials are marvellous plants for flower; by planting a succession of varieties you can have flowers virtually every month of the year, peaking in a magnificent pageant of colour through the summer. Many also possess attractive foliage, either as their sole feature or combined with flowers, and some even retain their foliage through winter.

Apart from taller varieties, which are best planted singly, perennials look most effective planted in groups; threes are usually sufficient in a small space. If you're looking to save money, buying one large plant and dividing it into three is an economical way of getting more plants. When your plants have developed into large clumps after several years, it's best to rejuvenate them by lifting and dividing the clumps, discarding the old centre and replanting the divisions. This is best done in autumn or early spring.

Most garden centres now stock a good selection of perennials – you'll find the best choice in autumn and spring. Less common varieties can be purchased from specialist nurseries, often by mail order.

Perennials are described in three main sections according to their preference for aspect: full sun; sun/part shade; and shade. Each section is subdivided into tall, medium and small perennials to help your border planning. Moisture-loving perennials are described on pages 124–5 and tender perennials on page 119. All sizes given below are those reached each year, once established.

PERENNIALS FOR FULL SUN

Unless stated otherwise, all perennials for full sun need a well-drained soil; some also do well in very dry soil.

The central feature of this garden is *Heuchera* 'Palace Purple' in a tall urn, seen here against the background of a dwarf pine.

TALL PERENNIALS – 1 M (3 FEET) AND ABOVE

Clematis are usually thought of only as climbers, but there are several unusual and very attractive herbaceous species. *Clematis heracleifolia* 'Wyevale' is an outstanding variety, forming a clump of large, palmate leaves and sending up stems bearing numerous clusters of up to 2 cm (¾ inch) wide, sky-blue flowers, with golden stamens, from late summer to mid-autumn. The flowers have a strong, hyacinth-like fragrance and are attractive to butterflies. *C.h.* var. *davidiana* is similar but with slightly smaller flowers. Height and spread 90 cm (3 feet).

Bees and moths love the flowers of *Echinops ritro* (globe thistle). This striking plant bears globular heads of steel-blue flowers in mid- to late summer on long stems adorned with jagged, grey-green leaves. It thrives on dry soils, including very chalky or sandy ones. Height 1.2 m (4 feet), spread 60 cm (2 feet).

Euphorbias are invaluable for architectural form and effect. One of my all-time favourites is *Euphorbia characias* subsp. *wulfenii*, which makes a superb feature plant, forming a bold clump of stems clothed in bluish-green leaves. Large heads of greenish-yellow, flower-like bracts, produced in early spring, are retained well into summer. Flowered stems should then be removed at ground level, leaving the new stems for winter colour. Beware the milky sap on this and

Herbaceous perennials can be real eye-catchers. The blue-green foliage on the right belongs to *Euphorbia wulfenii*, and contrasts well with the feathery plumes of an astilbe. White lilies in pots add an elegant touch.

all euphorbias, which can irritate the skin. This plant does well in sun or partial shade and on all except wet soils; it is especially good on dry soil. Height 1–1.2 m (3–4 feet), spread 0.6–1 m (2–3 feet). *E. griffithii* 'Fireglow' has smaller, brilliant orange-red bracts in early summer, which make a colourful display along with the dark olive-green foliage. It does well in sun or partial shade and prefers good, fertile soil that isn't too dry. Height 1 m (3 feet), spread 60 cm (2 feet).

A bold plant for rapid height is *Foeniculum vulgare* var. *purpureum* (bronze fennel), a handsome, easily grown plant producing tall stems covered in feathery, bronze-green foliage, which has a strong, aniseed scent and can be used for culinary purposes. In summer the stems are topped with flat heads of tiny, yellow flowers, which attract hover-flies – they look like wasps but are harmless to humans – their larvae are great aphid-eaters. Fennel self-seeds readily so cut off the heads before seed ripens, unless you want the seeds for culinary uses. Bronze fennel does especially well on dry soils and looks lovely planted with *Humulus lupulus* 'Aureus' (golden hop). Height 1.8 m (6 feet), spread 60 cm (2 feet).

MEDIUM PERENNIALS – 0.3–1 M (1–3 FEET)

Achilleas are reliable and colourful performers bearing flat heads of long-lasting flowers on tall stems in summer, above feathery, aromatic foliage. *Achillea* 'Moonshine' carries pale yellow flowers and attractive silver-grey foliage while *A.* 'Coronation Gold' boasts brighter yellow flowers. Height 0.6–1 m (2–3 feet), spread 45 cm (18 inches).

In mid-summer *Agapanthus* (blue African lily) produces large, globular heads of blue flowers on long stems above clumps of green, strap-like leaves. This handsome perennial makes an excellent tub plant, and looks lovely associated with the silver foliage of plants such as artemisia and stachys. There are many good blue varieties including *A.* Headbourne Hybrids, and some white ones are also available. African lilies are often sold as boxed perennials, which I find rarely grow well; pot-grown plants are more reliable. Height 0.6–1 m (2–3 feet), spread 45 cm (18 inches).

The long-lasting, lemon-yellow, daisy flowers of *Anthemis tinctoria* 'E. C. Buxton' (golden marguerite) go well with agapanthus and are valuable for summer colour. Golden marguerite particularly likes dry soils and flourishes in hot weather when many other flowers are flagging. The feathery, green foliage makes a neat base for the flowers. Height and spread 60 cm (2 feet).

Iris germanica hybrids add form to a border, with their clumps of bold, sword-like leaves, and create an excellent contrast to rounded and prostrate plants. The colourful flowers of these bearded irises are borne on long stems and make a superb show in early summer. The huge variety of colours – white, cream, red, yellow, brown and purple – come in many unusual combinations. Height 60 cm (2 feet), spread 45 cm (18 inches). For foliage interest *I. pallida* 'Variegata' is very attractive with its fan-shaped clumps of green-and-white, striped leaves. *I. tectorum* 'Variegata' – another excellent variety – has broad, glossy leaves boldly striped cream and green. It keeps its foliage all year, and tolerates very dry conditions. (Some lovely moisture-loving irises are described on page 123.) Height and spread 30 cm (1 foot).

Several dwarf kniphofias are real charmers

DROUGHT-TOLERANT PLANTS FOR A SUNNY SITE

Dry summers and water shortages have brought a much greater awareness of using plants that prefer dry, sunny sites. Growing drought-tolerant plants is one of the most effective and rewarding ways of conserving water in the garden. They positively flourish in long periods of hot weather whilst many other plants wither in the heat. Good winter drainage is the key to success – drought-tolerant plants tolerate a surprising amount of frost provided they aren't in waterlogged soil.

TREES, SHRUBS AND CLIMBERS

Artemisia
   (see pages 39 and 108)

Berberis (see pages 48–9)

Caragana (see pages 29–30)

Caryopteris (see page 34)

Ceratostigma (see page 34)

Cistus (sun rose)
   (see page 35)

Convolvulus cneorum
   (see page 35)

Cotoneaster
   (see pages 27, 50, 68)

Dorycnium hirsutum
   (see page 35)

Euonymus (see page 54)

Fremontodendron
   (see page 77)

Fuchsia (see page 44)

Genista (see page 35)

Halimiocistus (see page 35)

Hebe (see page 36)

Helichrysum (see page 39)

Hypericum 'Hidcote'
   (see page 45)

Lavandula (see page 36)

Perovskia (see page 38)

Phygelius (see page 38)

Potentilla (see page 45)

Robinia 'Frisia'
   (see page 21)

Rosmarinus (see page 38)

Ruta (rue) (see page 43)

Santolina (see page 39)

Salvia officinalis (sage)
   (see page 43)

Yucca (see page 43)

HERBACEOUS PERENNIALS

Achillea (see page 87)

Anthemis (see page 87)

Bergenia (see page 99)

Echinops (globe thistle)
   (see page 86)

Euphorbia wulfenii and E.
   myrsinites
   (see pages 86 and 91)

Foeniculum (fennel)
   (see page 87)

Geranium
   (see pages 93, 95, 99)

Helianthemum (rock rose)
   (see page 109)

Iris tectorum 'Variegata'
   (see page 87)

Osteospermum
   (see page 119)

Penstemon (see page 90)

Sedum spectabile
   (see page 90)

Sisyrinchium striatum
   'Variegatum' (see page 91)

Stachys (see page 91)

The bold yellow-green heads of Euphorbia wulfenii and the bright yellow flowers of Achillea immediately catch the eye. The tall rounded flowers belong to the summer-flowering bulb Allium afltunense.

and far removed from the larger, sprawling 'red hot pokers' of the same genus. The dwarf varieties carry short flower spikes in subtle colours of cream, yellow, coral-pink or red. One of the most attractive is K. 'Little Maid', with its pale lemon-yellow flower spikes in autumn. Height 60 cm (2 feet), spread 45 cm (18 inches).

The leaves and flowers of *Nepeta* × *faassenii* (catmint) are sharply aromatic and have a magnetic attraction for cats. Catmint forms a spreading cushion of small, grey-green leaves covered in clusters of lavender-blue flowers right through summer. It looks lovely tumbling over a path edge or raised bed, associates particularly well with roses, and likes all but the poorest soils. Height and spread 45 cm (18 inches).

Penstemons are star performers in hot, dry summers, producing upright stems of many tubular flowers from early summer until late autumn on rounded bushes of evergreen foliage. They aren't hardy in severe winters, but grow easily from cuttings taken in summer – a few overwintered indoors are a good safeguard. *Penstemon* 'Garnet' carries deep wine-red flowers and is excellent with pale yellow flowers such as *Santolina rosmarinifolia* 'Primrose Gem'. *P.* 'Hidcote Pink' has soft salmon-pink flowers while those of *P.* 'Sour Grapes' are vivid purple. Height and spread 60 cm (2 feet).

One of the latest perennials to flower is *Schizostylis coccinea* (kaffir lily), which bears slender spikes of small, cup-shaped, red, pink or white flowers above clumps of broad, grassy foliage from late summer often into winter, weather permitting. It needs a good soil and plenty of moisture in summer to flower well. *S.c.* 'Mrs Hegarty' produces pale pink flowers and *S.c.* 'Major' is bright crimson. There are other forms of *S. coccinea* in shades of pink and also a white form. Height 45 cm (18 inches), spread 30 cm (1 foot).

Sedum spectabile forms a neat clump of fleshy, glaucous leaves, and in late summer produces flat heads of pink flowers popular with butterflies. *S.s.* 'Brilliant' has darker pink flowers while those of *S.* 'Autumn Joy' are rich pink darkening with age. These sedums look good with blue flowers such as *Caryopteris* and *Ceratostigma willmottianum*, and thrive on soils from normal to very dry. Height and spread 45 cm (18 inches).

SMALL PERENNIALS – UP TO 30 CM (1 FOOT)

Dianthus (pinks) are excellent for edging borders and paths, forming spreading clumps of narrow, greyish leaves and bearing many sweetly scented flowers in summer. They have been popular in gardens for centuries. The oldest varieties with their prettily laced, fragrant flowers are the clove carnations or gillyflowers of cottage gardens; they may be purchased from specialist nurseries. The group known as garden pinks, with double flowers in shades of red, pink and white, are widely available. Good varieties include, *D.* 'Doris', with pink flowers, and *D.* 'Mrs Sinkins' and *D.* 'White Ladies' both with pure white flowers. Height 23 cm (9 inches), spread 45 cm (18 inches). Devon pinks is a new group, which includes some unusual colours. My favourite is *D.* 'Devon Cream' with its pale creamy yellow flowers lightly flecked with pink. *D.* 'Devon Dawn' carries tangerine flowers splashed with a darker orange and *D.* 'Devon Delight' produces white flowers streaked with red. Height and spread 30 cm (1 foot).

Diascias are marvellous for summer colour, bearing many small sprays of pink flowers from early summer onwards. They are excellent for patio tubs as well as borders but they dislike very dry soils. Diascias aren't reliably hardy in severe winters, so grow them from cuttings as insurance – they're well worth the effort. Height and spread 30 cm (1 foot).

Euphorbia myrsinites is an unusual, prostrate plant that looks good all year, with long, trailing shoots covered in waxy, bluish leaves and small heads of lime-green bracts in spring. It loves dry situations and looks good at the front of the border or edging a raised bed. Height 15 cm (6 inches), spread 30–60 cm (1–2 feet). Another good foliage plant is *Origanum vulgare* 'Aureum' (golden marjoram) which is both edible and ornamental. It forms a spreading clump of bright golden foliage, tinged with green after mid-summer, when it also produces small,

pink flowers. Easily grown, it does well on all but the driest soils, and is happy in partial shade. Height 15 cm (6 inches), spread 30 cm (1 foot).

Scabiosa 'Butterfly Blue' is the best scabious for the small garden, producing masses of lavender-blue, 'pincushion' flowers on short stems through summer. As its name suggests, the flowers attract butterflies. It prefers fertile, limy soil, as does *S.* 'Pink Mist', which carries mauve-pink flowers. These I find rather muddy in colour and not as pretty. Height and spread 45 cm (18 inches).

Sisyrinchium striatum 'Variegatum' is a dainty plant forming small, neat clumps of iris-like leaves beautifully striped with cream and green. In summer it produces stems of tiny, creamy flowers. It prefers a sheltered site on any reasonable soil, and looks especially good surrounded by gravel. Height 30 cm (1 foot), spread 15 cm (6 inches).

Stachys byzantina 'Silver Carpet' (lamb's ears) forms mats of bright silver, woolly leaves, which are retained all year and make excellent ground cover. It's easily grown and does well on all soils excepting wet ground. Its habit, colour and texture make it a wonderful companion to a multitude of other plants, especially those with purple foliage such as heuchera, and those with brightly coloured flowers such as crocosmia. Height 30 cm (12 inches), spread 45 cm (18 inches).

PERENNIALS FOR SUN/PART SHADE

TALL PERENNIALS - 1 M (3 FEET) AND ABOVE

The elegant, hooded flowers of *Aconitum* (monkshood) have a rather chilling beauty – perhaps because all parts of this plant are poisonous. It's a superb perennial with varieties flowering in both early summer and autumn. Monkshood thrives in conditions from sun to full shade, preferring retentive soil. My favourite is *A. carmichaelii*, which carries clear Wedgwood-blue flower spikes in autumn and looks lovely paired with *Sedum spectabile*. Height 1.2 m (4 feet), spread 45 cm (18 inches).

Varieties of *Anemone* × *hybrida*, also known as *A. japonica* (Japanese anemones), are popular and reliable plants for late summer flower; they're often associated with cottage gardens but look attractive almost anywhere with their white or pink flowers borne on long stems. They may be invasive when established. *A.* × *h.* 'Honorine Jobert' has pure white flowers while those of *A.* × *h.* 'Queen Charlotte' are semi-double and rich pink. Height 1.2 m (4 feet), spread 60 cm (2 feet). Other excellent plants for late summer are *Asters* (Michaelmas daisies). Their long-lasting colourful flowers are popular with butterflies. Michaelmas daisies prefer sun or light shade, and grow well on any reasonable soil. Best of all is *A.* × *frikartii* 'Mönch', which bears masses of lavender-blue flowers on branching stems from mid-summer to mid-autumn. Height 1 m (3 feet), spread 45 cm (18 inches).

MEDIUM PERENNIALS - 0.3-1 M (1-3 FEET)

Astilbes produce their large, fluffy panicles of flowers in late spring and early summer and have attractive, divided leaves, which are good weed-smotherers. They thrive in moist or even boggy soils, but grow well on all except very dry soils. Of the many hybrids, some of the best are: *Astilbe* 'Bridal Veil' with its pure white flowers; *A.* 'Europa', pale pink; *A.* 'Rheinland', bright pink; and *A.* 'Fanal', deep crimson-red. Height 0.6–1 m (2–3 feet), spread 60 cm (2 feet). The most delicate of the lovely, smaller hybrids is *A.* 'Sprite', which has feathery spikes of soft pink flowers in summer. If you prefer brighter colours, *A. chinensis* 'Pumila' carries dense spikes of rosy pink flowers, also in summer. On moist soil, astilbes look especially good with the lush green foliage of hardy ferns and the large, handsome leaves of hostas. Plants such as irises with spiky leaves also make a very effective contrast. Height and spread 45 cm (18 inches).

In late summer and early autumn crocosmias give a colourful display with their many spikes of elegant, brightly coloured flowers, borne on long stems above clumps of slender, grassy foliage. They dislike very heavy clay or boggy soils. *Crocosmia* 'Emberglow' produces vivid orange-red flowers; those of *C.* 'Firebird' are similar but with pale orange markings. *C.* 'Jenny Bloom' is a warm yellow and *C.* 'Bressingham Beacon' carries bright orange-and-yellow flowers. Height 0.6–1 m (2–3 feet), spread 30 cm (1 foot). *C.* 'Citronella' and *C.* 'Solfatare', which bear very attractive, yellow flowers, aren't reliably hardy in colder areas. Crocosmias look best associated with paler colours that cool and accentuate their brightly-coloured flowers, such as the silvery foliage of *Hebe* 'Pagei' and *Artemisia* 'Powis Castle'.

Dicentra spectabilis (bleeding heart or lady's locket) is a charming plant producing graceful, arching stems hung with tiny, rosy red and white flowers in early summer. It likes a good, retentive soil and prefers a shady site in warmer areas. *D.s. alba* is a delicate, white variety. The divided, pale green foliage is particularly attractive, emerging early in spring and dying down in late summer. Height 60 cm (2 feet), spread 45 cm (18 inches).

Hardy geraniums are one of the most useful and tolerant of all perennials. They thrive in all but boggy soils, forming spreading clumps of weed-proof foliage and flowering for many weeks in summer. Geraniums look good almost anywhere, and associate especially well with irises and roses. From early summer *Geranium endresii* 'Wargrave Pink' bears bright pink flowers and *G.* 'Johnson's Blue' has lavender-blue ones. *G.* 'Russell Prichard' is one of the best varieties, producing its magenta-pink flowers continuously from early summer onwards; they

look superb against its spreading mat of grey-green leaves. Height 30–60 cm (1–2 feet), spread 60 cm (2 feet).

An easily grown, cheerful plant is *Geum* (avens), which produces rosette-like flowers on stems in early summer. It does well on any well-drained, fertile soil. *G.* 'Mrs Bradshaw' is glowing orange-red and *G.* 'Lady Stratheden' bright yellow; both have double flowers. Height 60 cm (2 feet), spread 45 cm (18 inches). *G.* × *borisii* carries large, single, vivid warm orange flowers. Height 30 cm (1 foot), spread 30 cm (1 foot). *G. rivale* is a charming species for moisture-retentive

An attractive group for a shady corner – a red-flowering *Polygonum* is underplanted with *Lamium galeobdolen* 'Variegatum'.

soil, bearing many nodding, coppery pink flowers in early summer. Height 45 cm (18 inches), spread 30 cm (1 foot).

Meconopsis betonicifolia (Himalayan blue poppy) has you hooked for ever once you've seen its vivid blue flowers, though it has exacting cultural requirements. I first saw it making a breathtaking display with deciduous azaleas at Inverewe gardens in Scotland. These blue poppies need a cool, lime-free soil that is moist but not boggy, and prefer dappled shade. The flowers are borne in early summer. Height 1–1.2 m (3–4 feet), spread 30 cm (1 foot). By contrast, *Phlox paniculata* is one of the easiest perennials to grow. Phlox are lovely, cottage-garden plants invaluable for late summer colour, bearing clusters of richly scented flowers on long stems. They prefer a good soil and dislike extremes of chalk or clay. Good varieties include *P.p.* 'Eva Cullum', which is clear pink with a darker centre, and *P.p.* 'White Admiral' with its pure gleaming white flowers. Height 1 m (3 feet), spread 45 cm (18 inches).

SMALL PERENNIALS – UP TO 30 CM (1 FOOT)

Alchemilla mollis (lady's mantle) is an invaluable plant that grows almost anywhere in sun or shade, excepting boggy soil. Both flowers and foliage are beautiful: the scalloped, fresh green leaves form a spreading cushion and collect dew in tiny, quicksilver pearls. In early summer a froth of feathery, greenish-yellow flowers are produced and last for weeks. This is a lovely plant to soften the edges of paving, but it does self-seed everywhere – fine if you have old paving where plants look good growing in cracks, but otherwise trim off the heads after flowering. Height and spread 45 cm (18 inches).

The small *Aster novi-belgii* hybrids are good performers; two of the best dwarf varieties are *A.n.* 'Little Pink Beauty', with its semi-double, rich pink flowers, and *A.n.* 'Jenny', which has double, bright red flowers. Height and spread 30 cm (1 foot).

Several of the small dicentras form

The blue flowers of *Lavandula* 'Munstead' on the right, contrast well with the bright yellow-green flowers of *Alchemilla mollis*.

spreading mounds of delicate, deeply divided leaves and bear locket-like flowers on short, upright stems in late spring and early summer. *Dicentra* 'Luxuriant' has glowing dark pink flowers. *D.* 'Stuart Boothman' boasts pink flowers and handsome, glaucous foliage while *D.* 'Snowflakes' produces pure white flowers. Height and spread 30 cm (1 foot).

Of the small hardy geraniums, one of the best is *Geranium renardii*, which forms a dense clump of attractive, grey-green, lobed and deeply veined leaves. It carries small, white flowers traced with violet in early summer. Height and spread 30 cm (1 foot). *G. wallichianum* 'Buxton's Blue' is excellent for edging and ground cover, producing masses of large, clear blue flowers with white centres right through summer. It looks particularly good with yellow flowers such as *Potentilla* 'Elizabeth'. Height 30 cm (1 foot), spread 60 cm (2 feet).

Heuchera 'Palace Purple' makes a striking, plant useful for edging, with its neatly overlapping, heart-shaped, bronze-purple leaves. The tiny, white flowers, borne on thin, wiry stems from early summer onwards, are of secondary interest but still attractive. *H.* 'Rachel' also has bronze-purple leaves and produces coral-pink flowers. These varieties dislike very dry or wet soils. Height 30 cm (1 foot), spread 45 cm (18 inches).

Neat, spreading clumps of small evergreen leaves are formed by *Viola cornuta* (horned violet), which is covered with tiny, bright violet-blue flowers through summer. *V.c.* 'Alba' looks lovely with its glistening white flowers shown off against its glossy leaves. *V. cornuta* is excellent for edging and for underplanting shrubs such as *Daphne odora* 'Aureo-marginata'.

Waldsteinia ternata is a valuable carpeting plant for a dark corner, with dark, glossy, lobed leaves usually retained all year round and yellow, 'buttercup' flowers in spring. It likes a retentive soil. Height 10 cm (4 inches), spread 60 cm (2 feet).

PERENNIALS FOR SHADE

There are few bright colours to be found amongst shade-loving plants, but their beauty is subtle and long-lasting, provided by handsome foliage and paler flowers. Shady borders suit many of the best foliage plants, and most of the plants here also do well in partial shade.

TALL PERENNIALS - 1 M (3 FEET) AND ABOVE

Cimicifuga simplex 'White Pearl' (bugbane) is an unusual, autumn-flowering perennial producing slender, white, 'bottle-brush' flowers on tall stems above elegant, divided foliage. It prefers a cool, shady site and moist soil. The white flowers of *C. ramosa* 'Atropurpurea' and *C.r.* 'Brunette' contrast in early autumn with their handsome purple leaves. Height 1.2 m (4 feet), spread 60 cm (2 feet).

Tricyrtis hirta (toad lily) has an off-putting name, but makes a striking display in early autumn with its small, unusually shaped flowers which are pale lilac, heavily spotted with dark mauve. They are borne in loose clusters on top of sturdy, upright stems clothed in shining green, pointed leaves. Toad lily likes a moisture-retentive, humus-rich soil. Height 1 m (3 feet), spread 60 cm (2 feet).

This small shady corner next to a terraced house has been ingeniously planted. Hostas and grasses in pots occupy the far corner and by the doorway, *Parthenocissus henryana* climbs up the wall.

MEDIUM PERENNIALS – 0.3-1 M (1-3 FEET)

Aruncus dioicus 'Kneiffii' (dwarf goat's beard) forms a clump of dainty, fern-like, fresh green foliage. Feathery plumes of creamy white flowers appear in early summer. This tolerant plant likes sun as much as shade, on dry or moist soil. Height 1 m (3 feet), spread 45 cm (18 inches). It should not be confused with *A. sylvester*, which is much larger and coarser.

In mid- to late spring *Brunnera macrophylla* carries bright blue, 'forget-me-not' flowers on delicate stems produced from the centre of a spreading clump of dark green, heart-shaped leaves. It provides good ground cover, and dislikes very dry soil. Height 45 cm (18 inches), spread 60 cm (2 feet).

An excellent plant thriving where little else will grow is *Euphorbia robbiae*, a real thug of a plant that even flourishes in dry soil choked with roots. It looks very good too, forming clumps of shiny, evergreen foliage topped with heads of bright yellowish-green flowers in early spring. Remove the flowered stems at ground level in summer. Don't be kind and give this plant a sunny site in good soil; it will only reward you by taking over your garden! Height and spread 45 cm (18 inches).

Hellebores are exceptionally lovely, albeit poisonous plants, that I would be hard put to do without, as they bring colour and form to the garden at the dreariest times of year.

Clumps of *Helleborus orientalis* with plum-purple flowers look wonderful in late winter with dwarf bulbs – drifts of yellow, winter aconites and gleaming white snowdrops.

The first varieties start flowering in the depths of winter. *Helleborus niger* (Christmas rose) produces its delicate, nodding, white flowers on short stems from early winter until early spring; protecting the emerging buds from harsh winter weather with a sheet of glass will pay dividends. Christmas rose likes a humus-rich soil in shade. Height and spread 30 cm (1 foot). *H. foetidus* (stinking hellebore) flowers during the same period. Don't be put off by its name –

it's a superb plant bearing clusters of bell-shaped, pale green flowers and retains its dark green leaves all year. They give off their strong smell only when crushed. Stinking hellebore looks good with shrubs that have coloured stems such as dogwood or with winter-flowering heathers. It's happy on either rich or poor soil. Height and spread 45 cm (18 inches). *H. corsicus* (also known as *H. argutifolius*) is an exceptionally handsome plant, forming a mound of bold, greyish-green leaves and bearing stems of many small, cup-shaped, pale green flowers in late winter and spring. Height and spread 60 cm (2 feet).

H. orientalis (Lenten rose) carries many elegant, open flowers on top of a loose sheaf of stems, which rise from a spreading base of bold, evergreen leaves. Its flower colours range from palest cream through to crimson, often lightly flushed with green. This is my favourite hellebore, flowering from as early as late winter and lasting well into spring. Beloved by sleepy bees on sunny, late winter days, it does well on all but boggy soils. Height and spread 45 cm (18 inches).

Best of all foliage perennials are hostas (plantain lilies), which boast bold, attractively coloured leaves and wonderful spikes of flowers in summer. They thrive in complete or partial shade on normal to boggy soils, but dislike very dry soil. They'll also grow in sun, but only in permanently moist soil. Slugs and snails find the leaves a gourmet feast so some protection is usually

Hostas are one of the most handsome foliage perennials with their large ribbed leaves and lilac flowers. In this tiny garden the planting is confined to cool colours which makes it appear larger.

needed, right from early spring when the shoots first start to emerge. I find growing hostas in tubs not only makes an unusual patio display but also seems to discourage all but the most tenacious slugs and snails. There's an enormous range of leaf shapes and colours: varieties such as *H. sieboldiana* 'Elegans' and *H.* 'Halcyon' have grey-blue leaves; some such as *H.* 'Thomas Hogg' or *H. crispula* are variegated with cream or white; while others such as *H.* 'Royal Standard' have green leaves, or gold leaves such as *H.* 'August Moon'. Height and spread 0.3–1 m (1–3 feet).

An attractive evergreen for all-year interest is *Iris foetidissima* 'Citrina' (Gladwin iris) which forms a handsome clump of shining, dark green leaves. Small, pale yellow flowers are borne in summer, but these are just a prelude to its autumn splendour, when the swollen seed pods peel back to reveal rows of bright orange seeds. The seeds last for weeks or months until taken by the birds. Gladwin iris thrives in any soil, including very chalky ground, and tolerates difficult sites such as dry soil under trees. Height 60 cm (2 feet), spread 45 cm (18 inches).

SMALL PERENNIALS – UP TO 30 CM (1 FOOT)

Bergenia (elephant's ears) is so called because of its leathery, rounded evergreen leaves, which form spreading, ground-covering clumps. The leaves often develop attractive autumn tints. Flower heads, borne on short stems through spring, appear in a range from pure white to bright rose-purple. Bergenias thrive in sun or shade, and also do well on dry soils. *B.* 'Silberlicht' (also known as 'Silver Light') and *B.* 'Bressingham White' have pure white flowers. Those of *B.* 'Abendglut' (also known as 'Evening Glow') are bright rose-red and *B.* 'Sunningdale' vivid rose-pink. Height 30 cm (1 foot), spread 60 cm (2 feet).

The foliage of epimediums is more subtly beautiful than that of bergenias. Epimediums form carpets of delicate, heart-shaped, green leaves, some tinted

The pink flowers of bergenias make a wonderful splash of spring colour, and their large, leathery leaves look good all year.

with red in spring. Many plants retain some foliage through winter. This is best trimmed off in late winter, however, so that the tiny, spring flowers may be fully appreciated. Epimediums prefer part or full shade in any reasonable soil and like plenty of leaf-mould. *Epimedium* × *rubrum* has leaves tinted red in spring and autumn and rose-pink flowers. *E. perralderianum* produces fresh green leaves and bright yellow flowers. Height 30 cm (1 foot), spread 45 cm (18 inches).

Geranium macrorrhizum is a reliable plant for ground cover, creating a spreading clump of light green foliage often tinted red in autumn. Pink flowers appear on short stems in late spring. Good in sun as well as shade, this species does well on poor soils. *G.m.* 'Ingwersen's Variety' has pale rose-pink flowers while those of *G.m.* 'Bevan's Variety' are dark crimson. Height 30 cm (1 foot), spread 60 cm (2 feet).

One of the best plants for early spring flower is *Pulmonaria* (lungwort). Its spikes of colourful flowers are carried in early to mid-spring. Most attractive are deep blue-flowered varieties such as *P. angustifolia* 'Azurea' and *P.a.* 'Munstead Blue'. Height and spread 30 cm (1 foot).

Tiarella (foam flower) is a lovely ground-cover plant for humus-rich soil in full or part shade. In early summer many tiny flower spikes arise from carpets of small, pointed, green leaves. The foliage looks good all summer. Height 23 cm (9 inches), spread 45 cm (18 inches).

9

GRASSES AND FERNS

Ornamental grasses and hardy ferns are marvellous garden plants that are at last beginning to achieve the popularity they deserve. Foliage can easily become a neglected aspect of the garden in favour of flowers, but the sheer grace and delicacy of grasses and ferns plants can add a whole new feel to the garden, either when mixed with other plants or as harmonious grouping on their own.

GRASSES

Grasses add real style to the garden with their graceful foliage and ornamental seed heads; in a mixed border, their fragile stems contrast well with the rigid outlines of shrubs and conifers. Large grasses make superb feature plants, and small varieties may also be grown in tubs as unusual patio plants. In winter their dead leaves and seed heads fade to the palest parchment gold, which adds an ethereal touch to the winter garden when rimed and silvered with frost.

Several small, golden-leaved grasses are perfect for grouping at the edge of a border. *Carex morrowii* 'Evergold' forms a neat clump of slender, dark green leaves brightly edged with yellow. Height 15 cm (6 inches), spread 30 cm (1 foot). *Milium effusum* 'Aureum' (Bowles' golden grass) has soft gold leaves that look at their best in spring and early summer; clouds of little straw-coloured flowers appear in mid-summer. Height 60 cm (2 feet), spread 30 cm (1 foot). My favourite is *Hakonechloa macra* 'Aureola' (Japanese golden grass) a striking plant creating cascading clumps of leaves brilliantly striped with gold. Its arching foliage is shown off to perfection edging a raised bed or in a tub. Height 30 cm (1 foot), spread 45 cm (18 inches). One of the best variegated grasses is *Molinia caerulea* subsp. *caerulea* 'Variegata', which forms neat clumps of narrow, arching leaves boldly striped with cream and green. It looks lovely in flower too, holding its brownish-yellow,

Ferns and grasses cover a mostly-shady corner with a mass of luxuriant foliage. Ferns in particular are immensely useful for underplanting larger shrubs and trees, which grow to create a canopy of shady foliage.

feathery flowers on fine, creamy stems. Height 60 cm (2 feet), spread 30 cm (1 foot). All the above varieties prefer a good, retentive soil in part shade.

If you fancy something unusual try *Ophiopogon planiscapus nigrescens* (Japanese black grass). This makes spidery clumps of flat, narrow, black leaves and bears little sprays of purplish flowers in late summer. It likes partial shade and tones well with pink- or purple-flowered plants such as *Helleborus orientalis* (Lenten rose). Height and spread 30 cm (1 foot).

For sunny, sheltered sites, *Pennisetum* varieties are some of the loveliest flowering grasses. Most striking is *P. orientale* , which forms a dense clump of narrow, green leaves above which the unusual flower spikes are borne in mid-summer. These pale 'bottle-brushes' or 'long-haired caterpillars' later dry to a pale brown, thereby creating a stunning display until autumn. *P. orientale* looks lovely with summer-flowering perennials such as *Sedum spectabile* and *Aconitum* (monkshood). Height and spread 45 cm (18 inches).

There are several spectacular, larger grasses that make an eye-catching display, and one of the best for flower is *Deschampsia caespitosa* 'Golden Veil' (tufted hair grass). By mid-summer it carries many tall plumes of flowers, green at first but both stems and flowers soon turn golden-yellow, looking like trapped sunlight. This dense-clumped grass with arching, dark green leaves likes good, retentive soil and sun or light shade. Height 1.2 m (4 feet), spread 60 cm (2 feet).

Miscanthus sinensis varieties are marvellous plants forming tall, erect clumps of graceful foliage that make an excellent foil to other plants, and rustle soporifically in the lightest breeze. They are fairly easy to grow, liking any reasonable soil in sun or part shade and look particularly good associated with water. Several varieties produce attractive flowers as well as foliage. *M.s.* 'Silver Feather' has narrow, soft green leaves and, in late summer, bears many silken, arching sprays of pale brown flowers tinged with pink. *M.s.* 'Morning Light' is similar with leaves attractively edged with creamy white. *M.s.* 'Zebrinus' (zebra grass) is an eye-catching variegated grass with leaf blades banded with yellow by mid-summer; it also carries many flower sprays in autumn. Height 1.2–1.5 m (4–5 feet), spread 60 cm (2 feet).

FERNS

Ferns were a passion with the Victorians who grew hundreds of different varieties, but since those glory days ferns have been out of fashion; only recently have they become popular again. Their lush, fresh foli-

The eye is immediately drawn to the clump of Japanese black grass amongst a carpet of ivy in a raised bed. On the far wall a terracotta motif surrounded by the common white jasmine can be seen through a vine-clad archway.

age is an asset to any garden, and their liking for shade makes them ideal for freshening up a town garden or courtyard. Ferns look good with many shade-loving plants such as hellebores, hostas and *Alchemilla mollis.* Spring bulbs in-between the plants give a burst of early colour, and the ferns and perennials then grow to conceal the dying bulb foliage.

Hardy ferns aren't the sensitive creatures they're generally believed to be. Although most ferns need a humus-rich soil – heavy clay or chalk is definitely out of bounds – there are several varieties that happily flourish in drier soil so long as they're sheltered from cold winds and in part or full shade. However, no fern will give of its best in soil that is dry for long periods of time.

Of the varieties tolerant of drier conditions, one of the best is *Dryopteris filix-mas* (male fern). Thriving in fairly dry soil and disliking boggy ground, it forms a graceful 'shuttlecock' of divided leaves, which appear in spring curled up like snail shells and gradually unfurl to their full beauty. Its elegant shape can be seen at its best planted singly or in small groups, and amongst carpeting plants such as *Vinca minor* (periwinkle). Height 1 m (3 feet), spread 60 cm (2 feet).

A cobblestone and rock water feature is edged with tall clumps of *Miscanthus,* an ornamental grass with attractive variegated foliage. Their slender leaves provide a perfect contrast for the bold rounded leaves and bright yellow-orange flowers of *Ligularia* 'Desdemona', and a small hosta on the far left.

Excellent under trees and shrubs is the good, spreading, ground-cover fern *Polypodium vulgare,* with its deeply divided leaves. Old leaves are best trimmed off in spring so that the new foliage can be fully appreciated. Height and spread 30 cm (1 foot). *Polystichum setiferum* (soft shield fern) is one of the most elegant and luxuriant of all hardy ferns, tolerant of conditions from fairly dry to boggy soil. *P.s.* 'Acutilobum' produces dainty, dark green fronds, which are finely divided and grow in a spiral fashion from the crown. Height and spread 60 cm (2 feet).

Many lovely ferns need a reasonably moisture-retentive soil. Most exquisite is *Athyrium niponicum* 'Pictum' (Japanese painted fern) which has delicate, silvery leaves and purplish stems, the purple spreading out to stain the base of the fronds. *A. filix-femina* (lady fern) bears lacy, fresh green fronds, which look best in spring and summer; it will also grow on drier soils if sheltered from the winds. The feathery foliage of *Adiantum pedatum* is held on wiry, dark stems, similar to the maidenhair ferns popular as houseplants. *Phyllitis scolopendrium,* also known as *Asplenium scolopendrium* (hart's-tongue fern) is a handsome plant that forms open clumps of wavy, strap-shaped leaves that are bright glossy green. This is the fern so often seen putting out fresh tongues of foliage from Cornish stone hedges. Height and spread 30–60 cm (1–2 feet).

10

ALPINES AND HEATHERS

ALPINES

The small-scale beauty of alpine plants is perfectly in keeping with a small garden. The term 'alpine', which describes plants that are very dwarf, tends to give the impression they need a rockery in order to flourish, but alpines actually do well in a wide variety of sites around the garden so long as the soil is well drained. The tiniest plants look best in tubs, troughs and miniature rockeries; slightly larger varieties are good for rockeries, scree and raised beds; and the more vigorous varieties can be used in mixed borders, where they make excellent edging and ground cover on a small scale.

Although there are many different alpines ranging from popular and easily grown plants to very choice and more difficult varieties, only the more popular ones will be looked at here. The majority combine well with other compact plants: dwarf shrubs and conifers, heathers, and many of the exquisite little, spring bulbs. A few invasive varieties may become a nuisance in a small space and are best avoided, particularly *Euphorbia cyparissias*, *Polygonum vacciniifolium*, *Cerastium tomentosum*, the popular, grey-leaved snow-in-summer of old gardens, and some of the more vigorous sedums such as *S. acre*.

ALPINES FOR TUBS AND TROUGHS

The most essential requirement for growing alpines in containers is good drainage. Containers must have adequate drainage holes; when planting, the base should first be covered with a 5 cm (2 inch) layer of material such as broken clay pots, followed by a layer of rough, fibrous material such as coarse leaf-mould, which prevents the compost from seeping into the drainage layer. After planting, finish with a layer of fine chippings to improve the overall appearance and pre-

Alpines and other dwarf plants are perfect for gardening on a tiny scale. Plants with interesting foliage include the silvery mounded *Artemisia schmidtiana* 'Nana' and a *Sempervivum* with purple leaves. Flowers include cerise and orange helianthemums.

vent rain-splashed soil dirtying the plants.

Many lovely plants are suitable for containers. *Campanula* (bellflowers) are showy and invaluable plants covered in masses of white or blue, bell-shaped flowers throughout summer. Varieties of *C. carpatica*, *C. garganica* and *C. pusilla* are all especially good, and like sun or light shade. Height and spread 10 cm (4 inches). Also throughout summer, many delightful, small varieties of *Dianthus* (pinks) form little mats of grey foliage covered with colourful flowers, mostly in shades of red or pink. They love a well-drained, sunny site. Good varieties include *D.* 'Pike's Pink', with its double, pink, scented flowers, and *D.* 'Little Jock', which carries semi-double, rich pink flowers. Ideal to hang over the sides of a tub or trough are *Phlox douglasii* varieties, whose carpeting foliage is smothered in white, pink, mauve or red flowers in spring. Height 5 cm (2 inches), spread 15 cm (6 inches).

Saxifrages, with their attractive flowers and foliage, also make striking container plants. Some have unusual encrusted or rosetted leaves such as *S. paniculata*, height and spread 5–15 cm (2–6 inches), whilst others are grown for their flowers. *Sempervivum* (houseleeks) are handsome foliage plants with their large, striking rosettes of fleshy leaves in shades of green, bronze and red. They love a dry, sunny site. Height and spread 15 cm (6 inches). Thyme is suitable not only for tubs and troughs but can also be used in association with paving, either between slabs or as an edging plant. It has tiny, aromatic leaves in a range of colours; many prostrate spreading varieties will trail successfully over the edge of a container. Spread 15 cm (6 inches).

All the above varieties are fairly easy to grow, but there are a couple of enticing, popular varieties with more specialized needs. Gentians are almost irresistible with their trumpet-shaped, rich blue flowers, though they do need an acid, reasonably moisture-retentive soil. Height 5 cm (2 inches), spread up to 30 cm (1 foot). Lewisias seem to be on sale almost everywhere. Their eye-catching flower heads in many lovely shades of pink, red, white or yellow are borne on short stems above rosettes of foliage. However, they are relatively short-lived and prefer a neutral, fairly free-draining soil in sun; they detest having water gathered in their leaves for any length of time, so are best planted either at an angle or given protective covering in the wettest months. Height and spread 15 cm (6 inches).

ALPINES FOR ROCKERIES AND RAISED BEDS

For larger areas such as rockeries and raised beds, the choice of alpines widens considerably. Among those with attractive foliage are *Artemisia schmidtiana* 'Nana', with its spreading mounds of silver, lacy foliage, height 8 cm (3 inches), spread 20 cm (8 inches) and *Raoulia hookeri* which forms flat carpets of minute, silvery leaves. There are also many different sedums with gold, grey, red or purple foliage. Spread 25 cm (10 inches).

The choice of flowering alpines is immense. For good, reliable colour some of the best plants include: *Armeria maritima* (thrift) with red or white flowers, height 10 cm (4 inches), spread 15 cm (6 inches); *Geranium cinereum, G. dalmaticum* and *G. lancastriense* with white, pink or crimson flowers, height up to 15 cm (6 inches), spread 30 cm (1 foot); *Gypsophila repens*, which creates mats covered in pink flowers, height 5 cm (2 inches), spread 30 cm (1 foot); and *Veronica prostrata* with carpets of blue flowers, height 10 cm (4 inches), spread 30 cm (1 foot). All the above flower in late spring or summer. One of my favourite alpines is *Lithodora diffusa* 'Heavenly Blue' (also known as *Lithospermum*). Its spreading carpet of small, green leaves is covered with masses of tiny, deep gentian-blue flowers for weeks in summer. It needs a lime-free soil that is rich in humus but well-drained. Height 10 cm (4 inches), spread 30 cm (1 foot).

ALPINES FOR MIXED BORDERS

The spreading foliage of a number of the more vigorous alpines is ideal for the edge of a mixed border, softening paths or paving, or for raised beds and banks. Most flower in spring and early summer and are ideal for brightening up a mixed planting.

Alyssum saxatile, arabis and aubrieta are old favourites for reliable, spring colour. The bright golden-yellow flowers of *Alyssum saxatile* are set off well by its grey-green foliage; *A.s.* 'Citrinum' has more subtle, lemon-yellow flowers. Height 23 cm (9 inches), spread 30 cm (1 foot). *Arabis caucasica* varieties display white or pink flowers, and *A. ferdinandi-coburgii* 'Variegata' produces silver- or golden-variegated foliage – good for year-round interest. Height 5 cm (2 inches), spread 30 cm (1 foot). Although aubrietas come in many different colours, it's only worth buying named varieties; those propagated from seed generally have inferior flower colours. Height 8 cm (3 inches), spread 30 cm (1 foot).

Ajugas are excellent carpeting plants happy in either shade or sun, though they do dislike dry soil. Those with coloured foliage are most handsome; the leaves of *Ajuga reptans* 'Burgundy Glow' are suffused with red and pink, while those of *A. reptans* 'Atropurpurea' are reddish-purple. Both bear short spikes of blue flowers in summer. Height 15 cm (6 inches), spread 60 cm (2 feet). Also invaluable for dry, sunny sites are *Helianthemum* (rock roses). Throughout summer they bear masses of colourful flowers in white, cream, yellow, pink, red or orange. Their small, pointed leaves are green or grey; the grey-foliaged varieties in particular look very good. Height 23 cm (9 inches), spread 45 cm (18 inches). *Hypericum polyphyllum* also likes a dry, sunny site; it produces many bright yellow, 'pincushion' flowers in summer on a low mound of foliage, and looks lovely tumbling over the edge of a wall. Height 15 cm (6 inches), spread 30 cm (1 foot).

Iberis sempervirens (candytuft) is another old favourite alpine. It forms a spreading mound of dark, evergreen foliage and is smothered in glistening white flower heads in spring. Height 15 cm (6 inches), spread 45 cm (18 inches). *Leucanthemum hosmariense* is a real charmer, bearing white, golden-centred, daisy flowers above feathery, silver foliage; it likes sun and well-drained soil. Height 15 cm (6 inches), spread 30 cm (1 foot). *Lysimachia nummularia* 'Aurea' (golden creeping jenny) is also good as a permanent-tub or hanging-basket plant. Its soft, golden foliage makes good ground cover to brighten a damp or shady site, and the long, trailing stems are studded with yellow flowers in summer. Spread 45 cm (18 inches).

HEATHERS

Heathers are exceptionally good plants for all seasons, providing long-lasting colour with their attractive flowers and, in many cases, colourful foliage. Although some species need to be grown on acid soil, several of the best groups of species will grow happily in soil containing some lime. All heathers dislike very rich soil or boggy ground; they prefer plenty of leaf-mould and a mulch of

A combination of colourful flowers and foliage makes heathers ideal plants for a mixed border. Other plants include a golden dwarf pine and rhododendrons for spring colour. These summer-flowering heathers need an acid soil.

crushed bark to retain moisture, especially on lighter soils.

HEATHERS NEEDING ACID SOIL

Of those needing an acid soil, by far the largest group is *Calluna vulgaris*. This group falls into three flowering categories: early (mid- to late summer), mid-season (late summer to early autumn) and late (mid- to late autumn), so it's worth making sure you have a succession of flowers. Mostly forming low, rounded plants, they prefer sun or very light shade on a reasonably well-drained soil enriched with leaf-mould. There are many excellent varieties to choose from. A good proportion have coloured foliage that looks good all year: C.v. 'Beoley Gold', C.v. 'Blazeaway', C.v. 'Golden Carpet', C.v. 'Multicolor' and C.v. 'Robert Chapman'. Several bear green foliage tipped with cream, pink or red in spring: C.v. 'Spring Cream' and C.v. 'Spring Glow'. C.v. 'Velvet Fascination' and C.v. 'Silver Queen' boast attractive, silvery foliage. Many have stunning flowers backed by green foliage: C.v. 'Dark Star' carries dark pink flowers; C.v. 'H. E. Beale' with double, rose-pink ones; C.v. 'Kinlochruel' is a double white; and C.v. 'Red Star' with bright red flowers. Height and spread 30–45 cm (12–18 inches).

Several other groups need an acid soil: Erica cinerea, E. tetralix and E. vagans, which flower between early summer and mid-autumn. Daboecia varieties also need an acid soil. These charming, little plants bear many small urn-shaped flowers between early summer and late autumn. Height up to 45 cm (18 inches), spread 60 cm (2 feet).

LIME-TOLERANT HEATHERS

Erica carnea (winter heather) varieties are lime-tolerant and invaluable for brightening the garden in winter – most flower between mid-winter and early spring. They make a colourful, winter display with Cornus (dog-wood) with its red stems, and flowering perennials such as Helleborus foetidus. Several attractive, golden-foliaged varieties provide year-round interest, including E.c. 'Aurea', E.c. 'Foxhollow' and E.c. 'Ann Sparkes'. Otherwise most have green foliage and colourful flowers in all shades of pink, red or white. E.c. 'Myretoun Ruby' carries glowing rose-pink flowers, E.c. 'Springwood Pink' paler rose-pink ones while E.c. 'Vivellii' displays bright pink flowers against its bronzed, winter foliage. E.c. 'Springwood White' is a popular, white-flowering variety; a new variety E.c. 'Whitehall' is said to be as good with a neater, more compact habit. Height 15 cm (6 inches), spread 30–45 cm (12–18 inches).

E. × darleyensis is also winter flowering and grows a little taller and bushier than E. carnea. Although lime-tolerant it dislikes shallow chalk soils. E. × d. 'Kramer's Red' produces bright rose-pink flowers and E. × d. 'Silberschmelze' (also, confusingly, known as 'Alba' and 'Molten Silver') is white flowering. Height and spread 45 cm (18 inches). E. erigena varieties are spring flowering and also lime-tolerant. Height and spread 45 cm (18 inches).

All the above heathers are tough, hardy plants. One tender variety that has recently become popular is E. gracilis with its colourful spikes of white, pink or red flowers in early autumn. It makes a striking autumn bedding plant but doesn't tolerate frost.

11

ANNUALS, BIENNIALS
AND TENDER PERENNIALS

For a really glorious display of colourful flowers from late spring to autumn, nothing can beat annuals and tender perennials. These short-lived plants can be used in all sorts of places – tubs, borders, to infill between your permanent plants before they mature. In fact, anywhere there's a bit of bare soil or room to place a pot can be filled to make the garden as colourful as possible. It's well worth growing some of your favourite annuals in pots, so when your borders begin to look a bit tired in late summer, you can simply drop in a colourful tub of flowers.

ANNUALS

There are so many different varieties that I'm not going to describe individual ones, especially as it's very much a matter of personal taste whether you like flaming colours or subtle shades. Virtually every garden centre carries a good range of seeds, and a number of excellent seed firms send out their colourful catalogues on request. These normally arrive in winter – just when you need a good session of armchair gardening to lose yourself in visions of summer.

Many annuals can easily be grown from seed and are a cheap, very effective way of providing masses of summer colour. Some are beautifully scented: *Matthiola bicornis* (night-scented stock) and *Nicotiana* (tobacco plant) should be planted around patios and windows, where their sweet evening fragrance can be fully appreciated. Height 45–60 cm (18–24 inches), spread 30 cm (1 foot). *Reseda odorata* (mignonette) emits a delicious, musky scent, and no fragrant garden would be complete without the delicate perfume of sweet peas. Height 30–60 cm (1–2 feet), spread 30 cm (1 foot).

HARDY ANNUALS

Hardy annuals are best sown directly into the ground – usually around early spring –

Annuals and tender perennials add lots of colour to an otherwise dull garden. *Impatiens* (busy lizzies) thrive in the shadier areas on the left, while geraniums flourish on the right. *Diascia vigilis* with pale pink flowers tumbles over the edge of the wall.

unless the soil is very wet and cold, in which case they can be sown indoors in pots. If you're on a light soil, it's worth risking an autumn sowing, which can get plants off to a very early start.

Hardy annuals are easy to grow; some of my favourites include *Nigella damascena* (love-in-a-mist), *Limnanthes douglasii* (poached egg flower) and *Eschscholzia californica* (Californian poppy). The majority like sun or light shade, but a few such as *Mimulus* (monkey flower) tolerate full shade so long as the soil isn't too dry.

HALF-HARDY ANNUALS

These won't survive any frost at all and need to be raised under protection – ideally in a greenhouse or on a sunny windowsill. They should be planted out only after all danger of frost has passed; in most areas this will be in late spring but in the coldest areas may be in early summer. Even then, a freak frost can sneak up in early summer, and on occasions I've rushed round the garden protecting newly planted treasures with sheets of newspaper or fine netting. Many of the bedding plants sold in great quantities by garden centres are half-hardy annuals. The garden centres seem to be stocking up earlier every year, and many people unknowingly buy half-hardy plants only to have them killed by frost. So don't buy your plants too early – let the garden centres have the hassle of protecting them!

Although most half-hardy annuals prefer a site in full or part sun, a few will flourish in shade providing the soil is good. These include *Impatiens* (busy lizzie), lobelia and *Begonia semperflorens*. Height and spread 15 cm (6 inches).

ANNUAL CLIMBERS

Annual climbers are invaluable in a small garden. Because of their rapid growth and flower they can be planted in all sorts of places, yet, as they only last for one season, they can be grown through other permanent plants with no danger of throttling their hosts. They can be used for infill colour on walls and fences while your permanent climbers and wall shrubs are young, on wooden buildings where permanent plants could hold moisture and damage the woodwork, or on tripods within the border.

Cobaea scandens (cup and saucer plant) is a rapid, late-flowering scrambler with bell-shaped, deep violet-purple flowers. Sow indoors in late winter to early spring for planting out in early summer. It likes full sun. In very mild areas cobaea is perennial. Height 4–5 m (13–16 ft).

Ipomoea tricolor 'Heavenly Blue', also known as *Convolvulus tricolor* 'Heavenly Blue' (morning glory), bears wonderful, sky-blue flowers, which can be up to 10 cm

Mature shrubs and conifers provide the backdrop to a wealth of annuals – yellow and pink begonias, red dahlias, geraniums and busy lizzies. Grasses define the border corners, and the hardy fern *Dryopteris filix-mas* flourishes under the conifers.

PLANTS FOR A COMPACT COTTAGE GARDEN

The typical image of an old-fashioned English cottage garden is of a riotous mass of colourful and fragrant flowers, all tumbled together in glorious informality. By choosing older-style plants, even the smallest plot can become a compact cottage garden, though a modern version should be built around a framework of trees and shrubs if you want year-round interest. In addition to the plants listed below, most annuals give a blaze of excellent summer colour, hardy ferns are good for shady spots, and bulbs shouldn't be forgotten – daffodils, snowdrops, crocus and a host of others for spring colour, followed by lilies and alliums in summer.

TREES

Amelanchier (snowy
  mespilus) (see page 23)

Laburnum (golden rain
  tree) (see page 26)

Malus (crab apples)
  (see pages 23, 27–8)

Prunus subhirtella and
  P. × yedoensis
  (see pages 26 and 30)

SHRUBS AND CLIMBERS

Artemisia
  (see pages 39 and 108)

Chaenomeles
  (see pages 67–8)

Clematis
  (see pages 68, 71–3)

Cotoneaster horizontalis
  (see page 68)

Daphne (see pages 43–4)

Jasminum
  (see pages 69 and 74)

Lavandula (see page 36)

Lonicera (honeysuckle)
  (see page 74)

Philadelphus (mock orange)
  (see page 45)

Rosa (old-fashioned and
  English varieties)
  (see pages 62–3)

Rosmarinus (see page 38)

Salvia (sage) (see page 43)

Santolina (cotton lavender)
  (see page 39)

Viburnum tinus (see page 46)

Vinca (periwinkle)
  (see page 51)

Weigela (see page 46)

Wisteria (see pages 74–5)

PERENNIALS AND ALPINES

Achillea (see page 87)

Alchemilla (lady's mantle)
  (see page 94)

Alyssum saxatile
  (see page 109)

Anemone × hybrida
  (see page 92)

Aster (Michaelmas daisy)
  (see pages 92 and 94)

Aubrieta (see page 109)

Dianthus (pinks)
  (see page 90)

Dicentra
  (see pages 93 and 95)

Geranium
  (see pages 93, 95, 99)

Geum (see page 93)

Hellebore (see page 97)

Iris (see page 87)

Nepeta (catmint)
  (see page 90)

Phlox (see page 94)

Pulmonaria (lungwort)
  (see page 99)

Sedum (see page 90)

Stachys (lamb's ears)
  (see page 91)

A riotous mass of flowers nearly obscures the path to this old seat, which is backed by a wall of fragrant honeysuckle. Here a permanent framework of shrubs and conifers gives the garden structure all year and provides a background to the many summer flowers, which include the tall spikes of foxgloves.

(4 inches) across. The flowers open in early morning and are finished by evening, but many new flowers are produced each day – it's great fun going out each morning to count how many flowers have opened. The hard seeds are best soaked overnight before sowing to speed germination. All parts of the plant are poisonous. Height 1.8 m (6 feet).

Lathyrus odoratus (sweet peas) are famed for their delicately fragrant flowers of many colours. They make excellent cut flowers, so you can have regular sweet-smelling posies for a vase. Plants they must always be dead-headed to ensure continual flowering. Sweet peas revel in full sun and a good moisture-retentive soil, and seed can be sown directly into the ground, or indoors in pots for an early start. Height 1.8 m (6 feet).

Tropaeolum perigrinum (canary creeper) is a fast scrambler covered in bright yellow flowers, which are prettily fringed at the edges. It needs a reasonably well-drained soil and prefers sun, although it tolerates some shade. Canary creeper is excellent growing through another plant, especially one with blue or purple flowers or foliage such as caryopteris or weigela. Height 2.4 m (8 feet). Children love the brightly coloured flowers and rapid growth of the popular, easily grown *T. major* (nasturtiums). Many different varieties are available, including fast-growing climbing ones. An added bonus is that all parts of the plant are edible: the leaves, for example, may be used in salads, and the flowers also for decoration. Height 1.5 m (5 feet).

The above are some of the easier and most rewarding annual climbers. If you fancy some of the less common, harder-to-grow yet attractive varieties, try some of the following: *Asarina barclaiana* and *A. scandens*; *Cardiospermum halicacabum*; *Ipomoea alba*; *Mina lobata* (also known as *Quamoclit lobata*); and *Rhodochiton atrosanguineum*. All are half-hardy.

BIENNIALS

Biennials are particularly good for creating a cottage-garden style riot of colour. This group includes some of our best-loved, old flowers such as wallflowers, sweet williams, honesty, and the delightful, scented, mauve flowers of *Hesperis matronalis* (dame's violet or sweet rocket). Height 75 cm (2½ feet), spread 45 cm (18 inches). They need to be sown in early summer to flower the following year. If you haven't got space to raise plants from seed, you can buy many varieties from garden centres as young plants in late summer and autumn.

TENDER PERENNIALS

Tender perennials are superb plants that flower unstintingly from late spring until autumn. They've only recently become widely available and are often described as 'patio' plants. Although they're perfect for containers, they can also be used anywhere in the garden in suitable conditions – most tender perennials being sun lovers. Some also love dry soils. Some varieties may survive the winter outdoors, but generally only in the very mildest areas. Elsewhere over-winter tender perennials in a frost-free greenhouse or conservatory. Many can be grown easily from cuttings taken in late summer, which can be overwintered indoors.

Argyranthemum (marguerites) are old favourites with their sparkling white, daisy flowers and feathery, green foliage. My preference is for the single-flowered varieties such as A. 'Jamaica Primrose' and A. 'Apricot Surprise', both coloured as their names suggest. There are also double-flowered, pink, white or yellow varieties. Height 30–60 cm (1–2 feet), spread 30–45 cm (12–18 inches).

For an unusual fragrance try *Cosmos atrosanguineus* (chocolate plant) whose flowers have a mouthwatering scent of dark chocolate – not a plant to have if you're on a diet! The velvety, dark maroon flowers are like miniature dahlias and are borne in late summer and autumn. Height 30–60 cm (1–2 feet), spread 30 cm (12 inches).

In a sunny, dry position *Osteospermum* (African daisy) will give a tremendous show of large, daisy-like flowers. I find the white-flowering varieties are lovely for the evening garden, as in the dusk their flowers have a wonderful luminosity. For unusual flower shape, try O. 'Whirligig', which has white flowers with spoon-shaped petals. O. 'Buttermilk' carries delicate, creamy yellow flowers. O. 'Stardust' is a new variety that is said to be hardy, though I've yet to test it in a hard winter. It bears large, purple-pink flowers above glossy green foliage. Height 30–60 cm (1–2 feet), spread 30 cm (12 inches).

These are just a few of the best; other excellent tender perennials include: *Felicia amelloides*, with its gorgeous small blue, daisy flowers; Gazanias, with larger flowers in shades of yellow or orange; and *Bidens*, which produces small, yellow daisy flowers and has a rather lax habit – ideal in a tub growing through a small shrub. *Convolvulus mauritanicus* is a trailing plant with blue flowers, ideal for edging tubs and in hanging baskets. Heliotrope bears large heads of deep purple flowers, which have a lovely 'cherry-pie' scent – popular with butterflies, too. Height 30–60 cm (1–2 feet), spread 30 cm (1 foot).

12

WATER GARDENING

Water adds a whole new dimension and sense of tranquillity to the garden. In a pond you can grow a variety of handsome, aquatic and marginal plants, which display immensely attractive flowers and foliage and which stay lush and fresh through the driest of summers.

Pond size and shape should be in keeping with your garden, and can be as small as a wooden half-barrel sunk in the ground. Above ground, a pond in a tub makes an unusual patio feature. If there are young children around any surface water can be a potential danger, but you can still have safe running water in the form of a cobblestone or millstone fountain.

Water is top priority if you want to attract wildlife. Birds and mammals come to drink and bathe, frogs, toads and water insects soon take up residence, though ornamental fish should be excluded from a wildlife pond as they'll make a meal of your tadpoles. At least one pond side should be gently sloping for easy access – if not, there should be an escape route for hedgehogs and amphibians, as thousands drown each year in steep-sided ponds.

Pond plants are divided into three main groups: aquatics, which need to be fully submerged; marginal plants, which require their roots in water; and poolside or bog plants, which must have soil that is constantly moist. Some plants fall into both the last two categories.

The position of a pond and its construction should be carefully planned. Aquatic plants need a reasonable amount of sun, and access to electricity is necessary if you want a pump or fountain. Most aquatic plants, however, dislike moving, churning water. If you're using concrete or a flexible liner to build your pond, incorporate underwater shelves so that plants are submerged at different depths – small water lilies 30–45 cm (12–18 inches) under water, and marginal

Although not in flower, these pond plants still look attractive – a rounded clump of *Caltha palustris*, a variegated iris and a water lily. Plants in the adjacent border include a tall bamboo, a clump of *Iris foetidissima* and the dark-leaved *Viburnum davidii*.

plants on shelves 20 cm (8 inches) deep. A pond should be at least 75 cm (30 inches) deep in one part of it so that the water doesn't freeze completely in winter.

Planting is best done in spring and early summer, when plants are just starting into growth and have all summer to become well established. Pond plants are often sold in mesh containers ready to place in your pond; if not available in this way, buy a perforated planting basket, line it with hessian and plant it using special aquatic soil or good, loamy, garden soil, finishing with a topping of fine gravel. Avoid using recently fertilized or manured garden soil, as nutrients encourage the growth of green algae.

AQUATIC PLANTS

Nymphaea (water lilies) are real favourites, and their exotic flowers floating on the water's surface are an enchanting sight. Many varieties, with their white, pink, red or yellow flowers, are too vigorous for a small pond. Even using the smallest ones, it's best to have only one water lily in a small pond. Good compact varieties include: *N. odorata* 'Minor' and *N. pygmaea* 'Alba', both white with prominent, gold stamens. *N. laydekeri* 'Lilacea' bears rose-pink, slightly scented flowers. *N.* 'Froebelii' carries striking, deep red blooms while those of *N. odorata* 'Sulphurea' are fragrant and sulphur-yellow. *N.* 'Indiana' produces orange-red flowers darkening with age. Planting depth 30–45 cm (12–18 inches)

below the surface of the water.

Another good, deep-water aquatic is *Nuphar pumila* (butterball or brandy bottle) which has rounded, pale yellow flowers. Unlike water lilies, it tolerates running water and shade. Planting depth 30–60 cm (1–2 feet). Don't confuse it with *N. lutea*, which is very vigorous. *Aponogeton distachyos* (water hawthorn) is a wonderful plant bearing showy, white, dark-centred flowers with a rich, vanilla scent, borne from spring to autumn amongst long, green leaves. However, it isn't reliably hardy in colder areas. Planting depth 30 cm (1 foot).

All forms of pond life need oxygen in the water to remain healthy, including ornamental fish. The best way to keep pond water clear and healthy is to place some oxygenating plants in the water, which continually give off tiny bubbles of oxygen during the day. They also help to prevent the build-up of green algae. The best varieties of oxygenating plants for a small pond are sold in bunches, and should be planted in containers and submerged at the bottom of the pond.

MARGINAL PLANTS

Most small ponds can accommodate several marginal plants, and the best overall effect is achieved by having a contrasting mixture of shapes and colours. Plants with bold, sword-like or grassy leaves, for example, look very good with small, bushier plants. Variegated foliage adds extra interest.

One of the earliest marginals to flower is *Caltha palustris* (kingcup or marsh marigold), a native wild flower in Britain. Its clusters of large, brilliant gold flowers are like large, luscious buttercups and are beautifully displayed against large, rounded, green leaves. I find the simple beauty of the single-flowered varieties much more attractive than the double ones. Kingcup is happy in boggy soil or shallow water. Height and spread 30 cm (1 foot). *Myosotis scorpioides*, also known as *M. palustris* (water forget-me-not), has simple and lovely flowers that make a wonderful partner for *Caltha palustris*. It forms a carpet of delicate, tiny, blue flowers in late spring and early summer, which spreads out to make a pool of blue across the water's surface. It also likes boggy soil or shallow water. Height 15 cm (6 inches), spread 45 cm (18 inches).

Queen of the water irises is *Iris laevigata* from Japan, which bears masses of soft, clear lavender-blue flowers that make a wonderful, mid-summer display against its pale green, spear-like leaves. *I.l.* 'Alba' is a lovely white variety. One to avoid is the green-leaved *I. pseudacorus* (yellow flag) which is very vigorous; *I.p.* 'Variegata', however, is a suitable and striking plant that has wide leaves striped with yellow and carries yellow flowers with brown markings. Height 60 cm (2 feet). *Butomus umbellatus* (flowering rush) is a handsome sight in mid-summer, too. It bears rose-pink flower heads on long stems amongst triangular, sword-like,

dark green leaves. Height 0.6–1 m (2–3 feet), spread 45 cm (18 inches). Also for summer colour plant *Mimulus* (musk flower or monkey flower) which flowers from late spring right through summer. The two most handsome varieties are *M. luteus* and *M. guttatus*, both of which produce yellow flowers splashed with brown or dark red. Height 30 cm (1 foot).

Pontederia cordata (pickerel weed) is lovely for both flower and foliage. Glossy, heart-shaped, green leaves are held in upright clumps, amongst which spikes of soft blue flowers are borne in late summer. Height 60 cm (2 feet), spread 45 cm (18 inches). Another plant with handsome leaves is *Sagittaria sagittifolia* (arrowhead), which aptly describes its leaf shape. In summer it produces attractive spikes of white, brown-centred flowers. Height 60 cm (2 feet), spread 30 cm (1 foot).

Some grasses make good marginals. *Glyceria maxima* 'Variegata' is a striking plant with arching leaves striped creamy yellow and young shoots tinted with pink in spring. *Spartina pectinata* 'Aureo-marginata' also has graceful leaves striped with yellow and bears flower spikes that are green flushed with purple. Height 1–1.2 m (3–4 feet), spread is limited to the size of the container. *Typha minima* (dwarf reedmace) is often mistaken for a bulrush, with its brown, poker-shaped flowers borne in summer above narrow, grassy foliage. Height 45 cm (18 inches), spread 30 cm (1 foot).

POOLSIDE OR BOG PLANTS

Poolside plants can be used to make the transition between garden and water, but they can also be grown anywhere in moist soil or in a bog garden. Many hardy ferns flourish in boggy soil, and *Lysimachia nummularia* (creeping jenny) with its flowers like golden pennies, is lovely planted around pond edges, as is the golden-leaved *L.n.* 'Aurea'. Height 5 cm (2 inches),

spread up to 60 cm (2 feet).

Many other handsome plants must also have moist soil in order to grow; they will thrive in sun or part shade so long as they have plenty of moisture. *Houttuynia cordata* 'Chamaeleon', for example, makes a real splash of colour with its bright foliage. As its name suggests, the heart-shaped, dark green leaves are vividly coloured with red, orange and yellow. When crushed, the leaves give off a fresh, pungent scent. Tiny, white

Poolside plants flourish in the moist soil at the pond's edge, and include *Hosta fortunei* with lilac flowers, and a pink astilbe. On the right is *Rhododendron yakushimanum* with its silvery leaves.

flowers appear in summer. *H. cordata* 'Chamaeleon' may be invasive, so if this could be a problem grow it separately in a container, as a marginal plant – the red tints in the foliage become more pronounced when its feet are in water. Height and spread 30 cm (1 foot).

Ligularias are one of the most handsome marginal plants. The bold, dark green or red-tinged leaves are mostly heart-shaped or rounded, and emerge early to form an attractive clump. Bright orange, daisy flowers are borne on stems up to 1.5 m (5 feet) high in summer. Good varieties include *Ligularia dentata* 'Desdemona', *L.d.* 'Othello' and *L.* 'Gregynog Gold'. Height and spread 60–90 cm (2–3 feet).

Moisture-loving primulas are usually referred to as bog primulas, and are amongst the most enticing of all poolside plants. One of my favourites is *Primula florindae* (giant Himalayan cowslip) which carries soft yellow flower heads up to 1 m (3 feet) high in early summer. They exude a delicious, light scent. *P. sikkimensis* has similar, smaller flowers. Spread 30–45 cm (12–18 inches). *P. denticulata* (drumstick primula) bears round heads of white, lavender or purple flowers on short stems, and is a good, reliable plant for early spring colour. Height 30 cm (1 foot), spread 15 cm (6 inches). A number of other species are collectively termed 'candelabra primulas' because of the way the flowers cluster up the stems. Of these *P. bulleyana* has pale orange flowers

and *P. pulverulenta* deep crimson-purple flowers. Height 45 cm (18 inches), spread 30 cm (1 foot). One little primula that really grabs the eye is *P. vialii*, with its unusual, little, poker-shaped flower spikes of purple topped with red, borne above neat rosettes of foliage in summer. Height 30 cm (1 foot), spread 15 cm (6 inches).

Rodgersias are handsome foliage plants that deserve a place in every garden. Their bold fans of bronze-green, ridged leaves look good from spring to autumn, and are topped by feathery flower plumes in mid-summer. Rodgersias like a rich, moist soil in sun or light shade. There are several varieties, all of which are excellent: *Rodgersia aesculifolia* has creamy flowers while *R. pinnata* 'Superba' produces pink flowers and heavily bronzed leaves. Height 0.6–1 m (2–3 feet), spread 60 cm (2 feet).

Trollius (globe flowers) are lovely for fresh spring colour, bearing many large, rounded flower heads, in orange or yellow, above clumps of divided leaves. *T.* 'Earliest of All' carries its pale yellow flowers first in the season, followed by *T.* 'Canary Bird', which is golden-yellow, and *T.* 'Orange Princess' with its striking orange-yellow flowers. Height 60 cm (2 feet), spread 45 cm (18 inches).

A number of herbaceous perennials described on pages 95–9 also revel in moist soil and make excellent poolside plants, particularly *Aruncus*, astilbes, *Cimicifuga*, and *Schizostylis*.

NURSERIES SUPPLYING PLANTS BY MAIL ORDER

ALPINES
W.E. Th. Ingwersen Ltd, Birch Farm Nursery, Gravetye, East Grinstead, W. Sussex RH19 4LE.
Siskin Plants, April House, Davey Lane, Charsfield, Woodbridge, Suffolk IP13 7QG.

AQUATICS AND MARGINALS
Stapeley Water Gardens Ltd, London Road, Stapeley, Nantwich, Cheshire CW5 7LH.

CLEMATIS
Treasures of Tenbury, Burford House, Tenbury Wells, Worcs WR15 8HQ.
The Valley Clematis Nursery, Willingham Road, Hainton, Lincoln LN3 6LN.

CONIFERS
Bressingham Gardens (Blooms), Bressingham, Diss, Norfolk IP22 2AB.

GRASSES AND FERNS
Bressingham Gardens (see Conifers).
Unusual Plants (Beth Chatto), White Barn House, Elmstead Market, Nr Colchester, Essex CO7 7DB.

HERBACEOUS PERENNIALS
Bressingham Gardens (see Conifers).
Unusual Plants (see Grasses and ferns).

ROSES
David Austin Roses, Bowling Green Lane, Albrighton, Wolverhampton WV7 3HB.
Find That Rose details who grows what, and is published by the British Rose Growers' Association, 303 Mile End Road, Colchester, Essex CO4 5EA.

SEEDS
Chiltern Seeds, Bortree Stile, Ulverston, Cumbria LA12 7PB.
Thompson & Morgan, London Road, Ipswich, Suffolk IP2 0BA.

TREES, SHRUBS AND CLIMBERS
Burncoose Nurseries, Gwennap, Redruth, Cornwall TR16 6BJ.
Notcutts Nurseries Ltd, Woodbridge, Suffolk. IP12 4AF.

Directory of Mail Order Gardening can be obtained from Green Issues, 50 Denison Road, Ealing, London W5 1NU.
The Plant Finder lists 55000 plants and where to buy them. Available in all good bookshops.

INDEX

Page numbers in *italic* refer to the illustrations

INDEX